You're Still Not the Boss of Me!

52 Secrets to Regain Your Sparkle

WEEKLY TIPS, TRICKS, AND TESTED TECHNIQUES TO REDISCOVER YOUR HAPPINESS

STACIE BOYAR, LMHC, MSED

The information contained in this book is not intended as a substitute for consulting with a healthcare professional. All matters pertaining to your mental and physical health should be supervised by a licensed health care provider.

Published by:

Namastacie

PARKLAND, FLORIDA

www.namastacie.net

Copyright © 2025 Stacie Boyar

ISBN-13: 979-8-218-74639-1

All Rights Reserved. No part of this book may be reproduced or transmitted in any form or by any means, electronic or mechanical, including photocopying, or by any information storage and retrieval system, except for the purpose of brief excerpts for articles, books or reviews, without the written permission of the author.

This book is dedicated to YOU!
May these pages inspire you
to cultivate a life filled with fun,
laughter, and lasting fulfillment.

Contents

Introduction 1

Happiness Hacks 3
    Get Grounding 3
    Affirmation and Mantra Moments 5
    Unhappiness Hole 6

Week 1. Talk to a Random Person 7

Week 2. Get Dressed Up 13

Week 3. Talk About Ideas, Not People 19

Week 4. A Sunday Well Spent Makes a Week Content 25

Week 5. Seek Inspiration in Expected Places ... 31

Week 6. See an Idea to Fruition 37

Week 7. Creativity Turns on Happiness 43

Week 8. Emotional Contagion 49

Week 9. Hopefulness 55

Week 10. Say No 61

Week 11. Cheer for Others 67

Week 12. Ask for Help 73

Week 13. Thank You, Future Me	79
Week 14. Emotional Dignity and Emotion Regulation	85
Week 15. Give Happiness to Others	91
Week 16. It's Never Too Late or Too Early	97
Week 17. Three Good Things	103
Week 18. Why Not Me?	109
Week 19. Find One Thing to Like About Everyone	115
Week 20. Fall in Love with Your Worst Feature	121
Week 21. No Expectations	127
Week 22. Find What Makes You Feel Light	133
Week 23. The Reframe Game	139
Week 24. Judgy	145
Week 25. Volunteer	151
Week 26. You Are Not Your Thoughts	157
Week 27. Visualization	163
Week 28. Forgiveness	169
Week 29. Morning Routine	175
Week 30. Nighttime Routine	181
Week 31. Gratitude	187
Week 32. Nature Bathing	193
Week 33. Self-Care	199

Week 34. Take Up Space ... 205

Week 35. Declutter ... 211

Week 36. Go That Way, Not This Way ... 217

Week 37. No Comparing ... 223

Week 38. Action = Happiness ... 229

Week 39. Thank-You Note Journal ... 235

Week 40. Bloom from Within ... 241

Week 41. Make a Choice (to Be Happy) ... 247

Week 42. Find the Joy ... 253

Week 43. People-Please...Pa-lease! ... 259

Week 44. What Can We Control? ... 265

Week 45. Appreciation ... 271

Week 46. Focus on the Good ... 277

Week 47. Overthinking Won't Change the Outcome ... 283

Week 48. Sleep Hygiene ... 289

Week 49. Overcome Limiting Beliefs ... 295

Week 50. Negativity-Free Diet ... 301

Week 51. Be Present ... 307

Week 52. Fake It Till You Make It ... 313

Conclusion ... 319

About the Authors ... 320

Introduction

Welcome to your personal journey toward happiness. This book is designed to be your companion in exploring what happiness means to you and how to cultivate it in your life. By reading and engaging in the activities in this book, you will uncover your unique path to joy, fulfillment, and happiness. You will learn how to identify what brings you joy, how to navigate personal challenges, and how to foster positive habits.

The book is designed to be your companion over the next 52 weeks, providing you with one actionable happiness tip each week. By committing to these weekly practices, you will transform your perspective, enrich your life, and find happiness. This journey is not about progress not perfection, so if you skip a day, just pick up where you left off next time. These weekly steps are designed to empower you in your own unique way. Here's to a year filled with growth, joy, and happiness!

Happiness Hacks

By integrating small, easy, and intentional practices into our everyday routines, we can shift our focus toward mindfulness, gratitude, and joy. Engaging in simple, actionable activities will reframe our thoughts, create a sense of fulfillment, and elevate our moods. Over time these happiness hacks will become easier, even automatic, leading to greater resilience and overall happiness.

Ideally, review each happiness hack before beginning a new chapter as a reminder of who is in charge. You are in charge, not your bossy brain!

Also, use the happiness hacks when:

- ✦ You feel like your bossy brain is starting to take over.
- ✦ You begin to feel down, unmotivated, or sad.
- ✦ You experience something that triggers you.

GET GROUNDING

Is your bossy brain trying to convince you that you are overwhelmed, stressed, or unhappy? Grounding helps to connect your mind and body to the present to reduce the noises in your monkey mind. One grounding technique you can try that takes only a minute and you can do anywhere is the 5-4-3-2-1 method.

Start by taking a deep breath and focus on your surroundings. Begin by noticing five things you see around you. Next, listen closely to four sounds surrounding you. Then, identify three scents in your vicinity. After that, identify two things you can touch. Finally, think about something you want to taste. By engaging your senses this way, you will ground yourself in the present moment, creating calm, tranquility, and happiness.

What are five things you see?

1. _____
2. _____
3. _____
4. _____
5. _____

What are four things you hear?

1. _____
2. _____
3. _____
4. _____

What are three things you smell?

1. _____
2. _____
3. _____

What are two things you can touch?

1. _____
2. _____

What is one thing you can (or want to) taste?

1. _____

△△△ AFFIRMATION AND MANTRA MOMENTS △△△

When practiced often, positive phrases and thoughts reframe our negative thinking, foster a positive mindset, and boosts happiness. Write down and recite positive affirmations and/or mantras that make you happy. Here are some examples:

"I grow and improve every day."

"I am valued."

"I belong."

_____
_____
_____
_____
_____
_____
_____
_____

Engaging in repeated positive self-talk has been proven to help regulate emotions, increase energy, and boost our moods. Take a moment to recite your affirmations or mantras when you wake up in the morning, throughout the day, and before you go to bed at night.

♡♡♡♡♡♡ UNHAPPINESS HOLE ♡♡♡♡♡♡

Our bossy brains can keep us in a comfortable, yet negative, spiral, loop, or hole. Recognizing that you are headed down the unhappiness hole is a great start. Continue by digging yourself out of this hole by naming the trigger and brainstorming how you can eliminate or reduce them.

What is the trigger?

_____
_____
_____
_____

How can you eliminate or reduce the trigger?

_____
_____
_____
_____

Focus on one small task at a time instead of feeling like you have to tackle everything at once. Be sure to celebrate each obstacle as this will reinforce a sense of achievement, growth, and happiness.

WEEK 1

Talk to a Random Person

There are times in life when one may feel discontent, lonely, and unhappy. This may happen after scrolling through social media as others share their filtered joys and adventures. Maybe it occurs after sitting alone for hours during a Zoom meeting. Or maybe you feel unhappiness after believing your negative and faulty thoughts. Thoughts and feelings are not reality—don't believe that bossy brain!

Happiness can come from the most unexpected places or people. Make it a point to talk to one stranger every day. It is remarkable how sharing a simple conversation can brighten your day and remind you that there is beauty in everything. Begin with a smile at someone in the elevator. Continue with a comment to someone in line at the grocery store. Try giving someone a compliment at the gym. Talk to someone about the weather at your local coffee shop. You will be pleasantly surprised at how willing, grateful, and interested strangers are in connecting with you.

Notice how you feel after each interaction. We are all social beings, even introverted ones, who thrive on connections and interactions with others. Through these encounters, you are guaranteed to notice your sparkle returning. By opening your heart and mind to those around you, you may discover new perspectives, shared giggles, or even form new friendships.

Try these tips THIS WEEK:

- Send someone a kind good morning text.
- Compliment someone while standing on a line.
- Ask someone a question at a store.
- Ask a neighbor how they are doing.
- Wave and smile to all you pass while on a walk.
- Ask someone an open-ended question.

- ✦ Call a friend using a video-calling app.
- ✦ Comment kindly on social media posts.
- ✦ Send a voice memo to a friend.
- ✦ Send someone a kind message on a social media app.
- ✦ Make a positive comment on an online community or message board.
- ✦ Write a nice comment on a restaurant receipt.
- ✦ Strike up a conversation with the waitstaff at a restaurant.
- ✦ Ask for help at the gym.
- ✦ Say please and thank you.
- ✦ Your idea: _____

✿✿✿✿✿✿ DAILY CHECK-IN ✿✿✿✿✿✿

Monday:

On a scale of 1–10, how are you feeling today? _____

What do you need, want, or desire to get you one point higher?

_____
_____
_____

What are you grateful for?

_____
_____
_____

Tuesday:

On a scale of 1–10, how are you feeling today? _____

What do you need, want, or desire to get you one point higher?

_____
_____
_____
_____

What are you grateful for?

_____
_____
_____
_____

Wednesday:

On a scale of 1–10, how are you feeling today? _____

What do you need, want, or desire to get you one point higher?

_____
_____
_____
_____

What are you grateful for?

_____
_____
_____
_____

▪ Thursday:

On a scale of 1–10, how are you feeling today? _____

What do you need, want, or desire to get you one point higher?

_____
_____
_____
_____

What are you grateful for?

_____
_____
_____
_____

▪ Friday:

On a scale of 1–10, how are you feeling today? _____

What do you need, want, or desire to get you one point higher?

_____
_____
_____
_____

What are you grateful for?

_____
_____
_____
_____

WEEKLY RECAP

What three things went well this week?

1. _____
2. _____
3. _____

What did I learn about myself this week?

_____
_____
_____
_____

What would I have done differently?

_____
_____
_____
_____

Which tips did I try this week?

_____
_____
_____
_____

What did I do this week that I would like to continue in the upcoming weeks?

_____
_____
_____
_____

\\\\\\\\\\\\\\\\ **JOURNAL ENTRY** ////////////////

Describe your perfect day in detail.

WEEK 2
Get Dressed Up

The way we start the day sets the tone for the rest of the day. We have all felt rushed some mornings as we frantically throw on clothes and rush out the door. Then we spend the rest of the day frazzled, overwhelmed, and even unhappy. Conversely, on the days we have selected an outfit the night before, maybe with a pop of color and some accessories, we feel more confident, relaxed, and happy.

Be determined to find the joy in the mundane by making small yet significant shifts. Consciously choose an outfit the night before that makes you feel confident and happy, and enables you to express yourself. Notice how you feel and carry yourself when you wear clothing and accessories that empower you. Observe how other people respond to your new confidence, energy, and happiness.

Who said that the joy of dress-up has to end in preschool? If you get up each day and dress with intention, you spark joy within yourself and those around you. Simply putting on an outfit that makes you feel good is a powerful reminder that happiness is a decision you can make each morning.

Try these tips THIS WEEK:

- Check the next day's weather
- Review the next day's schedule
- Lay out appropriate clothes the night before
- Take out your shoes, jewelry, and accessories the night before
- Wear clothing that is comfortable
- Wear clothing that makes you feel good
- Arrange clothing in an easily accessible place
- Wear what makes you feel good

- Dress like the world is your runway
- Be creative with your clothing choices
- Express your personality through your clothing
- Donate items that do not bring you joy
- Dress like who you want to be
- Put full outfits on hangers for grab-and-go ease
- Your idea: _____

✤✤✤✤✤✤ DAILY CHECK-IN ✤✤✤✤✤✤

Monday:

On a scale of 1–10, how are you feeling today? _____

What do you need, want, or desire to get you one point higher?

_____
_____
_____
_____

What are you grateful for?

_____
_____
_____
_____

■ Tuesday:

On a scale of 1–10, how are you feeling today? _____

What do you need, want, or desire to get you one point higher?

_____
_____
_____
_____

What are you grateful for?

_____
_____
_____
_____

■ Wednesday:

On a scale of 1–10, how are you feeling today? _____

What do you need, want, or desire to get you one point higher?

_____
_____
_____
_____

What are you grateful for?

_____
_____
_____
_____

Thursday:

On a scale of 1–10, how are you feeling today? _____

What do you need, want, or desire to get you one point higher?

_____
_____
_____
_____

What are you grateful for?

_____
_____
_____
_____

Friday:

On a scale of 1–10, how are you feeling today? _____

What do you need, want, or desire to get you one point higher?

_____
_____
_____
_____

What are you grateful for?

_____
_____
_____
_____

WEEKLY RECAP

What three things went well this week?

1. _____
2. _____
3. _____

What did I learn about myself this week?

_____
_____
_____
_____

What would I have done differently?

_____
_____
_____
_____

Which tips did I try this week?

_____
_____
_____
_____

What did I do this week that I would like to continue in the upcoming weeks?

_____
_____
_____
_____

JOURNAL ENTRY

Describe what makes you feel most inspired.

WEEK 3

Talk About Ideas, Not People

Engaging in discussions about ideas rather than people can enhance our happiness! Talking about people breeds gossip, negative discussions, and sometimes toxic environments. These types of discussions can lead to comparisons and resentments, which often distract us from our goal of happiness. This type of communication can leave us feeling empty, and nobody wants that.

Let's shift the focus from people to ideas. Discussing ideas can promote a sense of connection and shared interests with others. By talking about things that matter to you, you can find common ground with others, creating bonds that strengthen relationships. Sharing thoughts can also lead to feelings of excitement, which can elevate your mood. By prioritizing discussions that inspire you, your happiness will be enhanced as you develop a deeper connection with those around you.

Discuss some of these topics THIS WEEK:

- Life experiences
- Future aspirations
- Biggest challenges
- Learned lessons
- Social justice
- Music
- Books
- Travel
- Adventures
- Art
- Dreams
- Business ventures
- Memories
- Travel experiences
- Favorite foods
- Role models
- Your idea: _____

༄༄༄༄༄༄ DAILY CHECK-IN ༄༄༄༄༄༄

▪ Monday:

On a scale of 1–10, how are you feeling today? _____

What do you need, want, or desire to get you one point higher?

_____
_____
_____
_____

What are you grateful for?

_____
_____
_____
_____

▪ Tuesday:

On a scale of 1–10, how are you feeling today? _____

What do you need, want, or desire to get you one point higher?

_____
_____
_____
_____

What are you grateful for?

_____
_____
_____
_____

▪ Wednesday:

On a scale of 1–10, how are you feeling today? _____

What do you need, want, or desire to get you one point higher?

_____
_____
_____
_____

What are you grateful for?

_____
_____
_____
_____

▪ Thursday:

On a scale of 1–10, how are you feeling today? _____

What do you need, want, or desire to get you one point higher?

_____
_____
_____
_____

What are you grateful for?

_____
_____
_____

Friday:

On a scale of 1–10, how are you feeling today? _____

What do you need, want, or desire to get you one point higher?

_____
_____
_____
_____

What are you grateful for?

_____
_____
_____
_____

WEEKLY RECAP

What three things went well this week?

1. _____
2. _____
3. _____

What did I learn about myself this week?

_____
_____
_____
_____

What would I have done differently?

_____
_____
_____
_____

Which tips did I try this week?

_____
_____
_____
_____

What did I do this week that I would like to continue in the upcoming weeks?

_____
_____
_____
_____

TALK ABOUT IDEAS, NOT PEOPLE

\\\\\\\\\\\\\\\ **JOURNAL ENTRY** ///////////////

Describe something that made you smile or laugh this week.

WEEK 4

A Sunday Well Spent Makes a Week Content

Have you ever experienced the Sunday scaries? You know, that sense of dread at the end of the weekend, that melancholy feeling as you think about the week ahead or regret that you didn't accomplish enough over the last couple of days. These thoughts are stealing your happiness. Don't believe those thoughts; they're not the boss of you!

Spending your Sunday mindfully can influence your contentment and happiness in the upcoming week. You have the ability to set the tone and lay the groundwork for your entire week. Create some rituals for your Sunday that make you feel safe, secure, and happy.

The happiest people usually have their own routines, practices, and regimens that keep them that way.

Try these tips THIS WEEK:

- Write in a gratitude journal
- Binge-watch a show.
- Practice mindfulness.
- Cook comfort food.
- Take a nap.
- Talk to friends.
- Take a bubble bath.
- Paint.
- Go for a nature walk.
- Listen to a meditation app.
- Do a digital detox by spending time away from screens.
- Write a list of personal strengths.
- Pick out your clothes for the next day.
- Read for pleasure.
- Your idea: _____

⚜⚜⚜⚜⚜ DAILY CHECK-IN ⚜⚜⚜⚜⚜

▪ Monday:

On a scale of 1–10, how are you feeling today? _____

What do you need, want, or desire to get you one point higher?

_____
_____
_____
_____

What are you grateful for?

_____
_____
_____
_____

▪ Tuesday:

On a scale of 1–10, how are you feeling today? _____

What do you need, want, or desire to get you one point higher?

_____
_____
_____
_____

What are you grateful for?

_____
_____
_____
_____

▪ Wednesday:

On a scale of 1–10, how are you feeling today? _____

What do you need, want, or desire to get you one point higher?

_____
_____
_____
_____

What are you grateful for?

_____
_____
_____
_____

▪ Thursday:

On a scale of 1–10, how are you feeling today? _____

What do you need, want, or desire to get you one point higher?

_____
_____
_____
_____

What are you grateful for?

_____
_____
_____
_____

Friday:

On a scale of 1–10, how are you feeling today? _____

What do you need, want, or desire to get you one point higher?

_____
_____
_____
_____

What are you grateful for?

_____
_____
_____
_____

WEEKLY RECAP

What three things went well this week?

1. _____
2. _____
3. _____

What did I learn about myself this week?

_____
_____
_____
_____

What would I have done differently?

_____
_____
_____
_____

Which tips did I try this week?

_____
_____
_____
_____

What did I do this week that I would like to continue in the upcoming weeks?

_____
_____
_____
_____

A SUNDAY WELL SPENT MAKES A WEEK CONTENT

\\\\\\\\\\\\\\\\ **JOURNAL ENTRY** ////////////////

Describe how you can amplify happy moments throughout your day.

_____
_____
_____
_____
_____
_____
_____
_____
_____
_____
_____
_____
_____
_____
_____
_____
_____
_____
_____
_____
_____
_____
_____
_____

WEEK 5

Seek Inspiration in Expected Places

*S*eeking inspiration can significantly enhance happiness by fostering a sense of purpose, creativity, and connection.

Begin by thinking about something you have always wanted to do. Next surround yourself with people, things, and even pictures that inspire you to do it. Have you always dreamed of running a marathon? Go to a running store where you are surrounded by running paraphernalia and runners. Notice how you feel after you leave. Have you always dreamed of becoming an artist? Walk around an art store, go to a museum, and research differing art mediums. Notice how you feel after you do this. Have you always wanted to throw a dinner party for friends? Look up interesting recipes, walk around farmers markets, or make a Pinterest board with all your ideas. Notice how you feel after you do this.

Before you know it, your dreams will become your reality. By engaging with the world around us, we discover new and exciting paths to joy and fulfillment. Actively seeking inspiration is a powerful catalyst for happiness.

Try these ideas THIS WEEK:

- Write down your interests.
- Brainstorm ways to submerge yourself in these interests.
- Read books about this interest.
- Research your areas of interest.
- Watch movies/documentaries about you interest.
- Surround yourself with people of similar interests.
- Go to places that motivate you to pursue this interest.
- Observe others who are actively engaged in this interest.
- Ask questions about this interest.

- ✦ Follow your dreams.
- ✦ Create a vision board.
- ✦ Do not be swayed by others.
- ✦ Your idea: _____

✿✿✿✿✿✿ DAILY CHECK-IN ✿✿✿✿✿✿

▪ Monday:

On a scale of 1–10, how are you feeling today? _____

What do you need, want, or desire to get you one point higher?

_____
_____
_____
_____

What are you grateful for?

_____
_____
_____
_____

▪ Tuesday:

On a scale of 1–10, how are you feeling today? _____

What do you need, want, or desire to get you one point higher?

_____
_____
_____
_____

What are you grateful for?

_____
_____
_____
_____

Wednesday:

On a scale of 1–10, how are you feeling today? _____

What do you need, want, or desire to get you one point higher?

_____
_____
_____
_____

What are you grateful for?

_____
_____
_____
_____

Thursday:

On a scale of 1–10, how are you feeling today? _____

What do you need, want, or desire to get you one point higher?

_____
_____
_____
_____

What are you grateful for?

_____
_____
_____

▪ Friday:

On a scale of 1–10, how are you feeling today? _____

What do you need, want, or desire to get you one point higher?

_____
_____
_____
_____

What are you grateful for?

_____
_____
_____

WEEKLY RECAP

What three things went well this week?

1. _____
2. _____
3. _____

What did I learn about myself this week?

_____
_____
_____
_____

What would I have done differently?

_____
_____
_____
_____

Which tips did I try this week?

_____
_____
_____
_____

What did I do this week that I would like to continue in the upcoming weeks?

_____
_____
_____
_____

SEEK INSPIRATION IN EXPECTED PLACES

JOURNAL ENTRY

Describe your dreams for the future.

WEEK 6

See an Idea to Fruition

New ideas are exciting, but that feeling can be fleeting. However, seeing an idea to completion fosters a sense of accomplishment, satisfaction, and happiness. Accomplishments boost self-esteem, leading to a sense of purpose and fulfillment.

Anyone can have a great idea, but actually seeing your plan come to life raises you to a new level of happiness. The journey of bringing your thoughts to fruition can be as rewarding as the end result. Ultimately, seeing an idea through nurtures creativity and growth, but also greater happiness.

Try these steps THIS WEEK:

- Get creative as you brainstorm a new idea.
- Write down your goals.
- Create a plan of action.
- Collect any resources you may need.
- Go for it.
- Remain resilient.
- Adjust ideas if needed.
- Keep going.
- Keep going.
- Keep going.
- Admire your accomplishment!
- Your idea: _____

♚♚♚♚♚ DAILY CHECK-IN ♚♚♚♚♚

▪ Monday:

On a scale of 1–10, how are you feeling today? _____

What do you need, want, or desire to get you one point higher?

_____

_____

_____

_____

What are you grateful for?

_____

_____

_____

_____

▪ Tuesday:

On a scale of 1–10, how are you feeling today? _____

What do you need, want, or desire to get you one point higher?

_____

_____

_____

_____

What are you grateful for?

_____
_____
_____
_____

▪ Wednesday:

On a scale of 1–10, how are you feeling today? _____

What do you need, want, or desire to get you one point higher?

_____
_____
_____
_____

What are you grateful for?

_____
_____
_____
_____

▪ Thursday:

On a scale of 1–10, how are you feeling today? _____

What do you need, want, or desire to get you one point higher?

_____
_____
_____
_____

What are you grateful for?

_____
_____
_____
_____

Friday:

On a scale of 1–10, how are you feeling today? _____

What do you need, want, or desire to get you one point higher?

_____
_____
_____
_____

What are you grateful for?

_____
_____
_____
_____

WEEKLY RECAP

What three things went well this week?

1. _____
2. _____
3. _____

What did I learn about myself this week?

_____
_____
_____
_____

What would I have done differently?

_____
_____
_____
_____

Which tips did I try this week?

_____
_____
_____
_____

What did I do this week that I would like to continue in the upcoming weeks?

_____
_____
_____
_____

\\\\\\\\\\\\\\\\ **JOURNAL ENTRY** ////////////////

Describe your proudest accomplishment?

WEEK 7

Creativity Turns on Happiness

*L*et's force that bossy brain to get creative! Being creative allows us to rise above the depths of despair by fostering self-expression, connection, and innovation. By embracing your creative spirit, you will begin to notice a sense of healing, freedom, and even empowerment.

Creative pursuits have a way of transforming sadness into self-discovery and self-love. Creative endeavors encourage emotional expression, mindfulness, and perhaps most importantly the feelings of hope and possibility. Begin by brainstorming ways to be creative. Do not allow your mind to limit your ideas and do not be judgmental of your ideas—remember, your thoughts are not the boss of you.

Try some of these pursuits THIS WEEK:

- Paint.
- Draw.
- Write.
- Take photos.
- Journal.
- Collage.
- Dance.
- Play an instrument.
- Join a theater group.
- Take a pottery class,
- Learn to crochet or knit.
- Make a TikTok reel.
- Blog.
- Learn graphic design.
- Garden.
- Make a Pinterest board.
- Sign up for a photography workshop.
- Start a DIY or upcycling project.
- Your idea: _____

DAILY CHECK-IN

▪ Monday:

On a scale of 1–10, how are you feeling today? _____

What do you need, want, or desire to get you one point higher?

_____
_____
_____
_____

What are you grateful for?

_____
_____
_____
_____

▪ Tuesday:

On a scale of 1–10, how are you feeling today? _____

What do you need, want, or desire to get you one point higher?

_____
_____
_____
_____

What are you grateful for?

_____
_____
_____
_____

▪ Wednesday:

On a scale of 1–10, how are you feeling today? _____

What do you need, want, or desire to get you one point higher?

_____
_____
_____
_____

What are you grateful for?

_____
_____
_____
_____

▪ Thursday:

On a scale of 1–10, how are you feeling today? _____

What do you need, want, or desire to get you one point higher?

_____
_____
_____
_____

What are you grateful for?

_____
_____
_____
_____

▪ Friday:

On a scale of 1–10, how are you feeling today? _____

What do you need, want, or desire to get you one point higher?

_____
_____
_____
_____

What are you grateful for?

_____
_____
_____
_____

WEEKLY RECAP

What three things went well this week?

1. _____
2. _____
3. _____

What did I learn about myself this week?

_____
_____
_____
_____

What would I have done differently?

_____
_____
_____
_____

Which tips did I try this week?

_____
_____
_____
_____

What did I do this week that I would like to continue in the upcoming weeks?

_____
_____
_____
_____

JOURNAL ENTRY

What skill would you like to learn?

___
___
___
___
___
___
___
___
___
___
___
___
___
___
___
___
___
___
___
___
___
___
___
___

WEEK 8

Emotional Contagion

Emotional contagion is the interesting phenomenon in which individual's emotions mimic those around them. This explains why it is so important to be mindful of those you surround yourself with. Begin to notice how you feel after leaving a person's presence. Do you feel happy, motivated, and calm? Or do you feel drained, exhausted, and unhappy?

We have the power to choose who we would like to be around. Consciously choosing to be around those who share positivity such as joy, excitement, and laughter foster an environment conducive to happiness. Whereas, surrounding yourself with negative individuals can have detrimental effects on your well-being. Be sure to make good friendship choices in order to nurture your happiness.

On a scale of 1 (highly negative) to 10 (highly positive), rate how you feel during each of your interaction. Make it a point to spend more time with those you rate 6–10, and less time with those you rate 1–5. Notice how you feel.

Try these tips THIS WEEK:

- Evaluate your relationships
- Prioritize uplifting relationships
- Set boundaries
- Seek individuals with shared interests
- Attend a class, event, or networking activity that interests you
- Surround yourself with people you want to be like.
- Surround yourself with people who reflect how you want to feel.
- Surround yourself with people who inspire you,
- Surround yourself with people who have healthy habits.

- ✦ Find a mentor.
- ✦ Go outside your comfort zone.
- ✦ Practice positive self-talk.
- ✦ Your idea: _____

✤✤✤✤✤✤ DAILY CHECK-IN ✤✤✤✤✤✤

Monday:

On a scale of 1–10, how are you feeling today? _____

What do you need, want, or desire to get you one point higher?

_____
_____
_____
_____

What are you grateful for?

_____
_____
_____
_____

Tuesday:

On a scale of 1–10, how are you feeling today? _____

What do you need, want, or desire to get you one point higher?

_____
_____
_____
_____

What are you grateful for?

_____
_____
_____
_____

Wednesday:

On a scale of 1–10, how are you feeling today? _____

What do you need, want, or desire to get you one point higher?

_____
_____
_____
_____

What are you grateful for?

_____
_____
_____
_____

Thursday:

On a scale of 1–10, how are you feeling today? _____

What do you need, want, or desire to get you one point higher?

_____
_____
_____
_____

What are you grateful for?

_____
_____
_____
_____

▪ Friday:

On a scale of 1–10, how are you feeling today? _____

What do you need, want, or desire to get you one point higher?

_____
_____
_____
_____

What are you grateful for?

_____
_____
_____
_____

WEEKLY RECAP

What three things went well this week?

1. _____
2. _____
3. _____

What did I learn about myself this week?

_____
_____
_____
_____

What would I have done differently?

_____
_____
_____
_____

Which tips did I try this week?

_____
_____
_____
_____

What did I do this week that I would like to continue in the upcoming weeks?

_____
_____
_____
_____

\\\\\\\\\\\\\\\\ **JOURNAL ENTRY** ////////////////

Describe what you would do right now if you knew you couldn't fail.

WEEK 9

Hopefulness

Hope for the future wards off depression, sadness, lack of motivation, and most importantly contributes greatly to happiness. Hopefulness through future planning has a special way of enriching our lives, fostering greater connections, and even promotes resilience.

Create a mind space open to possibilities and future thinking. This hopeful mind space enables you to dream of what could be and motivates you to make those dreams a reality. As you continue to have hope for future events, you begin to feel lighter, joyful, and happy.

Try some of these ideas THIS WEEK:

- Plan a trip.
- Take an online course.
- Learn a new language.
- Go skating.
- Explore going on a cruise.
- Try a new restaurant.
- Have a picnic.
- Throw a party.
- Go to a movie.
- Learn a sport.
- Do a craft.
- Learn a new language.
- Paint a room.
- Color.
- Do pottery.
- Plant a garden.
- Make a vision board.
- Learn woodworking.
- Begin a collection.
- Visualize yourself doing something exciting.
- Your idea: _____

✣✣✣✣✣✣ DAILY CHECK-IN ✣✣✣✣✣✣

▪ Monday:

On a scale of 1–10, how are you feeling today? _____

What do you need, want, or desire to get you one point higher?

_____
_____
_____
_____

What are you grateful for?

_____
_____
_____
_____

▪ Tuesday:

On a scale of 1–10, how are you feeling today? _____

What do you need, want, or desire to get you one point higher?

_____
_____
_____
_____

What are you grateful for?

_____
_____
_____
_____

▪ Wednesday:

On a scale of 1–10, how are you feeling today? _____

What do you need, want, or desire to get you one point higher?

_____
_____
_____
_____

What are you grateful for?

_____
_____
_____
_____

▪ Thursday:

On a scale of 1–10, how are you feeling today? _____

What do you need, want, or desire to get you one point higher?

_____
_____
_____
_____

What are you grateful for?

_____
_____
_____
_____

▪ Friday:

On a scale of 1–10, how are you feeling today? _____

What do you need, want, or desire to get you one point higher?

_____
_____
_____
_____

What are you grateful for?

_____
_____
_____
_____

WEEKLY RECAP

What three things went well this week?

1. _____
2. _____
3. _____

What did I learn about myself this week?

_____
_____
_____
_____

What would I have done differently?

_____
_____
_____
_____

Which tips did I try this week?

_____
_____
_____
_____

What did I do this week that I would like to continue in the upcoming weeks?

_____
_____
_____
_____

HOPEFULNESS

\\\\\\\\\\\\\\\\\ JOURNAL ENTRY /////////////

Describe how your perfect day looks.

_____
_____
_____
_____
_____
_____
_____
_____
_____
_____
_____
_____
_____
_____
_____
_____
_____
_____
_____
_____
_____
_____

WEEK 10

Say No

Feeling overwhelmed, overscheduled, and over-obligated can contribute to unhappiness. Saying no is a powerful tool to help regain control of your personal desires and can also enhance your happiness. By saying no, you are not simply rejecting others requests of you, but you are affirming your personal values, needs, and priorities. This will allow you to take control of your life and increase your happiness.

As you begin to say no to undesirable activities by setting boundaries, you will notice higher self-esteem, stronger resilience, more satisfying relationships, and greater happiness. Remember, saying no is an important self-care practice, and self-care is not selfish.

Try these steps THIS WEEK:

- Be direct, yet polite.
- Use "I" statements.
- Be honest.
- Use humor.
- Remain positive.
- Keep your response short and simple.
- Offer a choice.
- Express gratitude.
- Your idea: _____

✧✧✧✧✧ DAILY CHECK-IN ✧✧✧✧✧

▪ Monday:

On a scale of 1–10, how are you feeling today? _____

What do you need, want, or desire to get you one point higher?

_____
_____
_____
_____

What are you grateful for?

_____
_____
_____
_____

▪ Tuesday:

On a scale of 1–10, how are you feeling today? _____

What do you need, want, or desire to get you one point higher?

_____
_____
_____
_____

What are you grateful for?

_____
_____
_____
_____

▪ Wednesday:

On a scale of 1–10, how are you feeling today? _____

What do you need, want, or desire to get you one point higher?

_____
_____
_____
_____

What are you grateful for?

_____
_____
_____

▪ Thursday:

On a scale of 1–10, how are you feeling today? _____

What do you need, want, or desire to get you one point higher?

_____
_____
_____
_____

What are you grateful for?

_____
_____
_____
_____

Friday:

On a scale of 1–10, how are you feeling today? _____

What do you need, want, or desire to get you one point higher?

_____
_____
_____
_____

What are you grateful for?

_____
_____
_____
_____

WEEKLY RECAP

What three things went well this week?

1. _____
2. _____
3. _____

What did I learn about myself this week?

_____
_____
_____
_____

What would I have done differently?

_____
_____
_____
_____

Which tips did I try this week?

_____
_____
_____
_____

What did I do this week that I would like to continue in the upcoming weeks?

_____
_____
_____
_____

\\\\\\\\\\\\\\\\\ **JOURNAL ENTRY** /////////////

Describe a time you said yes to a person when you would have rather said no.

_____
_____
_____
_____
_____
_____
_____
_____
_____
_____
_____
_____
_____
_____
_____
_____
_____
_____
_____
_____
_____
_____
_____
_____

WEEK 11

Cheer for Others

Always remember that being truly happy for other people's achievements will never diminish your own happiness or achievements. Being happy for others will only enhance it. Cheering for others significantly contributes to our happiness by strengthening bonds and positive interactions with others.

By routing for others, we shift the focus off of ourselves and onto others, which strengthens our self-esteem. Not only is this feeling liberating, but it also enables us to let go of negative emotions and develop a positive outlook. This form of positivity creates a positive atmosphere and energy that will invariably draw people to you.

Try some of these ideas THIS WEEK:

- Offer random heartfelt compliments.
- Send a thoughtful text.
- Actively listen (nod, say um hmm).
- Encourage others to follow a dream.
- Do a random act of kindness.
- Share with someone how they brightened your day.
- Attend events you are invited to.
- Be mindful of using positive language.
- Your idea: _____

♛♛♛♛♛♛ DAILY CHECK-IN ♛♛♛♛♛♛

▌ Monday:

On a scale of 1–10, how are you feeling today? _____

What do you need, want, or desire to get you one point higher?

_____
_____
_____
_____

What are you grateful for?

_____
_____
_____
_____

▌ Tuesday:

On a scale of 1–10, how are you feeling today? _____

What do you need, want, or desire to get you one point higher?

_____
_____
_____
_____

What are you grateful for?

_____
_____
_____
_____

▪ Wednesday:

On a scale of 1–10, how are you feeling today? _____

What do you need, want, or desire to get you one point higher?

_____
_____
_____
_____

What are you grateful for?

_____
_____
_____
_____

▪ Thursday:

On a scale of 1–10, how are you feeling today? _____

What do you need, want, or desire to get you one point higher?

_____
_____
_____
_____

What are you grateful for?

_____
_____
_____
_____

▪ Friday:

On a scale of 1–10, how are you feeling today? _____

What do you need, want, or desire to get you one point higher?

_____
_____
_____
_____

What are you grateful for?

_____
_____
_____
_____

WEEKLY RECAP

What three things went well this week?

1. _____
2. _____
3. _____

What did I learn about myself this week?

_____
_____
_____
_____

What would I have done differently?

_____
_____
_____
_____

Which tips did I try this week?

_____
_____
_____
_____

What did I do this week that I would like to continue in the upcoming weeks?

_____
_____
_____
_____

\\\\\\\\\\\\\\\\ **JOURNAL ENTRY** ////////////////

Describe when you felt happy for someone else.

_____
_____
_____
_____
_____
_____
_____
_____
_____
_____
_____
_____
_____
_____
_____
_____
_____
_____
_____
_____
_____
_____

WEEK 12

Ask for Help

Many people do not want to ask for help claiming that they don't want to rely on others, don't want to seem needy, or don't want to be thought of as a burden. However, this thought is not at all accurate. Others will feel valued, trusted, and appreciated if you ask them for a small favor. Moreover, asking for help will alleviate feelings of isolation, loneliness, and sadness. Showing vulnerability by asking for help from others fosters deeper levels of connection and greater happiness. When we are feeling down, we may feel as though we are navigating life alone. Don't believe that bossy brain. Ask for help and notice how you feel.

Try asking some of these questions THIS WEEK:

- How do I get to (*fill in the blank*)?
- Can you help me carry this?
- Will you text me the phone number for (*fill in the blank*)?
- Would you mind watching this for a moment?
- What time is it?
- What do you think about (*fill in the blank*)?
- Can I use your pen, please?
- Where would I find (*fill in the blank*)?
- Can you hold this for a minute?
- Will you grab that for me?
- Your idea: _____

✿✿✿✿✿ DAILY CHECK-IN ✿✿✿✿✿

▪ Monday:

On a scale of 1–10, how are you feeling today? _____

What do you need, want, or desire to get you one point higher?

_____
_____
_____
_____

What are you grateful for?

_____
_____
_____
_____

▪ Tuesday:

On a scale of 1–10, how are you feeling today? _____

What do you need, want, or desire to get you one point higher?

_____
_____
_____
_____

What are you grateful for?

_____
_____
_____
_____

■ Wednesday:

On a scale of 1–10, how are you feeling today? _____

What do you need, want, or desire to get you one point higher?

_____
_____
_____
_____

What are you grateful for?

_____
_____
_____
_____

■ Thursday:

On a scale of 1–10, how are you feeling today? _____

What do you need, want, or desire to get you one point higher?

_____
_____
_____
_____

ASK FOR HELP

What are you grateful for?

_____
_____
_____
_____

▪ Friday:

On a scale of 1–10, how are you feeling today? _____

What do you need, want, or desire to get you one point higher?

_____
_____
_____
_____

What are you grateful for?

_____
_____
_____
_____

WEEKLY RECAP

What three things went well this week?

1. _____
2. _____
3. _____

What did I learn about myself this week?

_____
_____
_____
_____

What would I have done differently?

_____
_____
_____
_____

Which tips did I try this week?

_____
_____
_____
_____

What did I do this week that I would like to continue in the upcoming weeks?

_____
_____
_____
_____

\\\\\\\\\\\\\\\\\ **JOURNAL ENTRY** /////////////

Describe a time you helped someone and how it made you feel.

_____
_____
_____
_____
_____
_____
_____
_____
_____
_____
_____
_____
_____
_____
_____
_____
_____
_____
_____
_____
_____
_____
_____
_____

WEEK 13

Thank You, Future Me

Remind yourself that your actions today will have an effect on your future self. We want our future selves to not only thank us but also be proud of us. If we gently remind ourselves of the consequences of our actions, we will begin to align our current goals with our future goals. It will soon be clear that immediate gratification isn't the road to future happiness.

Begin to make a conscious effort to align your current actions with future desires. Know that you have the willpower to be uncomfortable, patient, and strong in the moment. This will generate greater fulfillment, success, and happiness for future you. Prepare your future self for success.

Try these tips THIS WEEK:

- Eat healthy foods.
- Exercise.
- Save/invest your money.
- Practice mindfulness.
- Embrace a growth mindset.
- Attend a workshop, class, or conference.
- Prioritize self-care.
- Practice your organizational skills.
- Make a vision board.
- Act with intention.
- Make a to-do list and cross out entries when completed.
- Cultivate emotional intelligence.
- Practice emotion regulation.
- Develop an online presence.
- Practice visualizations.
- Use a budget.
- Build a professional network.
- Learn a new skill.
- Get that certification.
- Save for retirement.
- Your idea: _____

✿✿✿✿✿ DAILY CHECK-IN ✿✿✿✿✿

▪ Monday:

On a scale of 1–10, how are you feeling today? _____

What do you need, want, or desire to get you one point higher?
_____
_____
_____
_____

What are you grateful for?
_____
_____
_____
_____

▪ Tuesday:

On a scale of 1–10, how are you feeling today? _____

What do you need, want, or desire to get you one point higher?
_____
_____
_____
_____

What are you grateful for?

_____
_____
_____
_____

▪ Wednesday:

On a scale of 1–10, how are you feeling today? _____

What do you need, want, or desire to get you one point higher?

_____
_____
_____
_____

What are you grateful for?

_____
_____
_____
_____

▪ Thursday:

On a scale of 1–10, how are you feeling today? _____

What do you need, want, or desire to get you one point higher?

_____
_____
_____
_____

What are you grateful for?
_____
_____
_____

Friday:

On a scale of 1–10, how are you feeling today? _____

What do you need, want, or desire to get you one point higher?
_____
_____
_____

What are you grateful for?
_____
_____
_____

WEEKLY RECAP

What three things went well this week?

1. _____
2. _____
3. _____

What did I learn about myself this week?

_____
_____
_____
_____

What would I have done differently?

_____
_____
_____
_____

Which tips did I try this week?

_____
_____
_____
_____

What did I do this week that I would like to continue in the upcoming weeks?

_____
_____
_____
_____

THANK YOU, FUTURE ME

JOURNAL ENTRY

Describe your ideal future self.

___
___
___
___
___
___
___
___
___
___
___
___
___
___
___
___
___
___
___
___
___

WEEK 14

Emotional Dignity and Emotion Regulation

Emotional dignity is a fancy way of saying that we all want to feel heard, respected, and valued. Knowing that our feelings are valid, genuine, and important while respecting the emotions of others builds our emotional dignity and adds happiness to our lives. Once we recognize and are attentive to our feelings and the feelings of others, we can begin to mindfully self-regulate our emotions.

Here's a secret: those who can self-regulate their emotions are much happier and more successful in all of their interpersonal relationships. Begin by understanding your triggers while labeling the emotions you are feeling while triggered. Show dignity to your emotions by withholding judgment, negativity, or scrutiny. Accept the feeling and acknowledge where it is coming from. Talk to yourself kindly as if you were talking to your best friend. Achieving emotional dignity and emotion regulation is a journey that will ultimately foster happiness, strengthen your self-esteem, and create positive bonds with others.

Try these strategies THIS WEEK:

- Practice deep breathing.
- Practice grounding.
- Practice visualization.
- Practice mindfulness.
- Practice muscle-relaxation techniques.
- Practice positive self-talk.
- Get seven to nine hours of sleep each night.
- Respect personal space.
- Exercise.
- Be inclusive of others.

- Respect boundaries.
- Be nonjudgmental.
- Stick with your routine.
- Take a three-minute break periodically to move your body or practice self-care.
- Respect other people's decisions.
- Drink more water than you think you need.
- Journal.
- Your idea: _____

✤✤✤✤✤✤ DAILY CHECK-IN ✤✤✤✤✤✤

Monday:

On a scale of 1–10, how are you feeling today? _____

What do you need, want, or desire to get you one point higher?

_____
_____
_____
_____

What are you grateful for?

_____
_____
_____
_____

Tuesday:

On a scale of 1–10, how are you feeling today? _____

What do you need, want, or desire to get you one point higher?

_____
_____
_____
_____

What are you grateful for?

_____
_____
_____
_____

Wednesday:

On a scale of 1–10, how are you feeling today? _____

What do you need, want, or desire to get you one point higher?

_____
_____
_____
_____

What are you grateful for?

_____
_____
_____
_____

Thursday:

On a scale of 1–10, how are you feeling today? _____

What do you need, want, or desire to get you one point higher?

_____
_____
_____
_____

What are you grateful for?

_____
_____
_____
_____

Friday:

On a scale of 1–10, how are you feeling today? _____

What do you need, want, or desire to get you one point higher?

_____
_____
_____
_____

What are you grateful for?

_____
_____
_____
_____

🖾🖾🖾🖾🖾 WEEKLY RECAP 🖾🖾🖾🖾🖾

What three things went well this week?

1. _____
2. _____
3. _____

What did I learn about myself this week?

_____
_____
_____
_____

What would I have done differently?

_____
_____
_____
_____

Which tips did I try this week?

_____
_____
_____
_____

What did I do this week that I would like to continue in the upcoming weeks?

_____
_____
_____
_____

\\\\\\\\\\\\\\ **JOURNAL ENTRY** ////////////

Describe any obstacles you faced today and how you overcame them.

___

WEEK 15

Give Happiness to Others

Surprisingly enough, when we engage in acts of kindness, we not only uplift others but also boost our own happiness. Giving happiness to others creates joy, fulfillment, and satisfaction for all parties involved. This altruistic behavior also reduces stress, anxiety, and depression. When we shift our mindset from what we lack to what we can offer, our lives become more satisfying.

Create a ripple effect of positivity and happiness that will benefit you and those around you by spreading joy to others. When someone experiences an act of kindness, it uplifts their spirits and inspires them to pay it forward to others. This chain reaction enables all parties involved to feel more connected, appreciated, and happy.

Try these tips THIS WEEK:

- Compliment someone.
- Share a smile.
- Volunteer.
- Be an active listener (no peeking at phones).
- Pass along a funny meme or reel.
- Buy local.
- Cook a meal for someone.
- Offer to help a person in need.
- Share a skill.
- Organize a fun event.
- Send a thoughtful message.
- Take in a neighbor's trash.
- Thank the mail carrier.
- Your idea: _____

✧✧✧✧✧ DAILY CHECK-IN ✧✧✧✧✧

▪ Monday:

On a scale of 1–10, how are you feeling today? _____

What do you need, want, or desire to get you one point higher?
_____
_____
_____
_____

What are you grateful for?
_____
_____
_____
_____

▪ Tuesday:

On a scale of 1–10, how are you feeling today? _____

What do you need, want, or desire to get you one point higher?
_____
_____
_____
_____

What are you grateful for?

_____
_____
_____

▪ Wednesday:

On a scale of 1–10, how are you feeling today? _____

What do you need, want, or desire to get you one point higher?

_____
_____
_____
_____

What are you grateful for?

_____
_____
_____

▪ Thursday:

On a scale of 1–10, how are you feeling today? _____

What do you need, want, or desire to get you one point higher?

_____
_____
_____
_____

What are you grateful for?

_____
_____
_____
_____

Friday:

On a scale of 1–10, how are you feeling today? _____

What do you need, want, or desire to get you one point higher?

_____
_____
_____
_____

What are you grateful for?

_____
_____
_____
_____

WEEKLY RECAP

What three things went well this week?

1. _____
2. _____
3. _____

What did I learn about myself this week?

_____
_____
_____
_____

What would I have done differently?

_____
_____
_____
_____

Which tips did I try this week?

_____
_____
_____
_____

What did I do this week that I would like to continue in the upcoming weeks?

_____
_____
_____
_____

\\\\\\\\\\\\\\\\ **JOURNAL ENTRY** ////////////

Describe something that makes you smile.

_____
_____
_____
_____
_____
_____
_____
_____
_____
_____
_____
_____
_____
_____
_____
_____
_____
_____
_____
_____

WEEK 16

It's Never Too Late or Too Early

Changing perspectives allows individuals to embrace change, discover opportunities, and find happiness at any stage of life. By shifting our thoughts to an "it's never too late or too early mindset," we alleviate many societal pressures of when milestones are supposed to be met. This idea empowers us to live authentically without succumbing to ridiculous and burdensome time constraints.

It is extremely powerful to be reminded that growth and fulfillment are within reach, noting that growth and joy can happen at any age. Most importantly, the "it's never too late or too early mindset" encourages a positive outlook, promotes personal growth, and foster's connections—all of which are keys to happiness.

Try these THIS WEEK:

- Find a hobby.
- Volunteer.
- Practice a new self-care routine.
- Learn a new skill.
- Create a signature recipe.
- Try a new sport.
- Go back to school.
- Read a biography.
- Plant a garden.
- Explore a new career.
- Create an exercise routine.
- Get a library card.
- Become tech savvy.
- Take a walk.
- Your idea: _____

❦❦❦❦❦ DAILY CHECK-IN ❦❦❦❦❦

▪ Monday:

On a scale of 1–10, how are you feeling today? _____

What do you need, want, or desire to get you one point higher?

_____
_____
_____
_____

What are you grateful for?

_____
_____
_____
_____

▪ Tuesday:

On a scale of 1–10, how are you feeling today? _____

What do you need, want, or desire to get you one point higher?

_____
_____
_____
_____

What are you grateful for?

_____
_____
_____
_____

▪ Wednesday:

On a scale of 1–10, how are you feeling today? _____

What do you need, want, or desire to get you one point higher?

_____
_____
_____
_____

What are you grateful for?

_____
_____
_____
_____

▪ Thursday:

On a scale of 1–10, how are you feeling today? _____

What do you need, want, or desire to get you one point higher?

_____
_____
_____
_____

What are you grateful for?

_____
_____
_____
_____

▪ Friday:

On a scale of 1–10, how are you feeling today? _____

What do you need, want, or desire to get you one point higher?

_____
_____
_____
_____

What are you grateful for?

_____
_____
_____
_____

WEEKLY RECAP

What three things went well this week?

1. _____
2. _____
3. _____

What did I learn about myself this week?

_____
_____
_____
_____

What would I have done differently?

_____
_____
_____
_____

Which tips did I try this week?

_____
_____
_____
_____

What did I do this week that I would like to continue in the upcoming weeks?

_____
_____
_____
_____

\\\\\\\\\\\\\\\\ **JOURNAL ENTRY** ////////////////

Describe something you would like to do if timing wasn't a factor.

WEEK 17

Three Good Things

Finding three good things to focus on is an extremely effective way to enhance happiness. If we consciously focus on the beauty all around us, we appreciate the present moment, alleviate anxiety and depression, and find happiness.

When concerned about a new experience, such as entering a classroom, event, or office, find three beautiful things that grab your attention in that room. Allow those three things to monopolize your attention. Begin to notice your anxiety, depression, and unhappiness subside. Consciously focusing on something appealing is a powerful tool for managing depression. Finding mental distractions in your surroundings helps with emotion regulation, serenity, and happiness.

Look for beauty in these things THIS WEEK:

- A photo
- An illustration
- A sculpture
- Clouds
- A book
- A plant
- Artwork
- Beautiful fabrics
- Mountains
- Water
- Architecture
- Stained glass
- Children
- Animals
- Your idea: _____

⚜⚜⚜⚜⚜⚜ DAILY CHECK-IN ⚜⚜⚜⚜⚜⚜

▪ Monday:

On a scale of 1–10, how are you feeling today? _____

What do you need, want, or desire to get you one point higher?

_____
_____
_____
_____

What are you grateful for?

_____
_____
_____
_____

▪ Tuesday:

On a scale of 1–10, how are you feeling today? _____

What do you need, want, or desire to get you one point higher?

_____
_____
_____
_____

What are you grateful for?

_____
_____
_____
_____

▇ Wednesday:

On a scale of 1–10, how are you feeling today? _____

What do you need, want, or desire to get you one point higher?

_____
_____
_____
_____

What are you grateful for?

_____
_____
_____
_____

▇ Thursday:

On a scale of 1–10, how are you feeling today? _____

What do you need, want, or desire to get you one point higher?

_____
_____
_____
_____

What are you grateful for?

_____
_____
_____
_____

Friday:

On a scale of 1–10, how are you feeling today? _____

What do you need, want, or desire to get you one point higher?

_____
_____
_____
_____

What are you grateful for?

_____
_____
_____
_____

WEEKLY RECAP

What three things went well this week?

1. _____
2. _____
3. _____

What did I learn about myself this week?

_____
_____
_____
_____

What would I have done differently?

_____
_____
_____
_____

Which tips did I try this week?

_____
_____
_____
_____

What did I do this week that I would like to continue in the upcoming weeks?

_____
_____
_____
_____

\\\\\\\\\\\\\\\\ JOURNAL ENTRY /////////////

Describe in your body where you feel happiness?

WEEK 18

Why Not Me?

Beginning a new task, starting a job, or doing something we've never done before can be daunting. Our bossy brains may try to talk us out of forging ahead. It may say things like "You're not qualified," "You don't know what you're doing," and "You'll get laughed at." However, we're in the business of not always believing our monkey minds! An extremely powerful tool is reframing those thoughts.

Begin by shifting your mindset from "Why me?" to "Why *not* me?!" Truth be told, people way less qualified than you are doing what you want to be doing. Do you know why? They didn't believe their bossy brains and took action. You can, too! Pay attention to those negative "Why me?" thoughts, then challenge them. Ask yourself what concrete evidence you have to support that thought. Perhaps those thoughts are based in fear not facts. Then visualize yourself successfully completing that goal. Take that visualization even farther by envisioning yourself successfully completing the task and receiving much deserved praise.

Try these tips THIS WEEK:

- Ask for a raise, promotion, new office.
- Learn a new skill.
- Take a risk in your relationship.
- Plan a solo trip.
- Make an appointment.
- Repair something.
- Start a business.
- Make a TikTok video.
- Design a website.
- Take a class.
- Teach a class.
- Apply for a job.
- Make a TED talk.

- ✦ Learn yoga.
- ✦ Write a book.
- ✦ Audition for a play.
- ✦ Your idea: _____

✿✿✿✿✿ DAILY CHECK-IN ✿✿✿✿✿

▪ Monday:

On a scale of 1–10, how are you feeling today? _____

What do you need, want, or desire to get you one point higher?

_____
_____
_____
_____

What are you grateful for?

_____
_____
_____
_____

▪ Tuesday:

On a scale of 1–10, how are you feeling today? _____

What do you need, want, or desire to get you one point higher?

_____
_____
_____
_____

What are you grateful for?

_____
_____
_____
_____

▪ Wednesday:

On a scale of 1–10, how are you feeling today? _____

What do you need, want, or desire to get you one point higher?

_____
_____
_____
_____

What are you grateful for?

_____
_____
_____
_____

▪ Thursday:

On a scale of 1–10, how are you feeling today? _____

What do you need, want, or desire to get you one point higher?

_____
_____
_____
_____

What are you grateful for?

_____
_____
_____
_____

■ Friday:

On a scale of 1–10, how are you feeling today? _____

What do you need, want, or desire to get you one point higher?

_____
_____
_____
_____

What are you grateful for?

_____
_____
_____
_____

WEEKLY RECAP

What three things went well this week?

1. _____
2. _____
3. _____

What did I learn about myself this week?

_____
_____
_____
_____

What would I have done differently?

_____
_____
_____
_____

Which tips did I try this week?

_____
_____
_____
_____

What did I do this week that I would like to continue in the upcoming weeks?

_____
_____
_____
_____

\\\\\\\\\\\\\\\\ **JOURNAL ENTRY** ////////////////

Describe something you've always wanted to learn and why.

___

WEEK 19

Find One Thing to Like About Everyone

A great way to nurture a sense of fulfillment, joy, and happiness in your life is to find one thing to like about everyone. At times we may find ourselves around people who are difficult and unpleasant to engage with. We may focus or fixate on their unbecoming behaviors. Focusing on the negative characteristics will not foster happiness, and that's our goal!

By shifting your perspective to look for likable qualities, you will develop an appreciative and positive mindset rather than a critical and judgmental one. Another exciting trait you will notice by observing the positive in others is an immediate reflection on you. This mirror effect will contribute to greater self-worth, self-esteem, and happiness.

Notice some of these traits in challenging people THIS WEEK:

- A sense of humor
- Creativity
- An act of kindness
- A differing perspective
- A thoughtful act
- A talent
- Good energy
- A nice smile
- A passion
- A pretty outfit
- Story-telling ability
- Helpful
- A hearty laugh
- Strength
- Confidence
- A pleasant perfume/cologne
- Good posture
- Hard work
- Your idea: _____

ꙮꙮꙮꙮꙮ DAILY CHECK-IN ꙮꙮꙮꙮꙮ

▪ Monday:

On a scale of 1–10, how are you feeling today? _____

What do you need, want, or desire to get you one point higher?

_____
_____
_____
_____

What are you grateful for?

_____
_____
_____
_____

▪ Tuesday:

On a scale of 1–10, how are you feeling today? _____

What do you need, want, or desire to get you one point higher?

_____
_____
_____
_____

What are you grateful for?

_____
_____
_____
_____

▪ Wednesday:

On a scale of 1–10, how are you feeling today? _____

What do you need, want, or desire to get you one point higher?

_____
_____
_____
_____

What are you grateful for?

_____
_____
_____
_____

▪ Thursday:

On a scale of 1–10, how are you feeling today? _____

What do you need, want, or desire to get you one point higher?

_____
_____
_____
_____

What are you grateful for?

_____
_____
_____

▪ Friday:

On a scale of 1–10, how are you feeling today? _____

What do you need, want, or desire to get you one point higher?

_____
_____
_____

What are you grateful for?

_____
_____
_____

WEEKLY RECAP

What three things went well this week?

1. _____
2. _____
3. _____

What did I learn about myself this week?

_____
_____
_____
_____

What would I have done differently?

_____
_____
_____
_____

Which tips did I try this week?

_____
_____
_____
_____

What did I do this week that I would like to continue in the upcoming weeks?

_____
_____
_____
_____

FIND ONE THING TO LIKE ABOUT EVERYONE

\\\\\\\\\\\\\\\\ **JOURNAL ENTRY** ////////////////

Describe a specific moment that made you like a person.

WEEK 20

Fall in Love with Your Worst Feature

Why is it so easy to focus on the negative instead of the positive? Let's stop listening to that bossy brain right now! Embracing and loving what we consider our worst feature will lead to self-acceptance, resilience, and happiness. When we accept and love our flaws, we become more authentic.

The ultimate trick to happiness is unabashedly being your complete and authentic self. Practice speaking kindly to yourself. You may even consider putting positive sticky notes on your mirror to look at and recite each morning.

Tell yourself some of these positive things THIS WEEK:

- I am unique.
- I am capable.
- I am joy.
- I am proud of myself.
- I am resilient.
- I am beautiful inside and out.
- I am worthy.
- I am constantly improving each day.
- I deserve happiness.
- I am confident.
- I am enough.
- I am a good person.
- I am special.
- I am light.
- I am liked.
- I am deserving.
- I am strong.
- I am likeable.
- Your idea: _____

⚜⚜⚜⚜⚜ DAILY CHECK-IN ⚜⚜⚜⚜⚜

▪ Monday:

On a scale of 1–10, how are you feeling today? _____

What do you need, want, or desire to get you one point higher?

_____
_____
_____
_____

What are you grateful for?

_____
_____
_____
_____

▪ Tuesday:

On a scale of 1–10, how are you feeling today? _____

What do you need, want, or desire to get you one point higher?

_____
_____
_____
_____

What are you grateful for?

_____
_____
_____
_____

▪ Wednesday:

On a scale of 1–10, how are you feeling today? _____

What do you need, want, or desire to get you one point higher?

_____
_____
_____
_____

What are you grateful for?

_____
_____
_____
_____

▪ Thursday:

On a scale of 1–10, how are you feeling today? _____

What do you need, want, or desire to get you one point higher?

_____
_____
_____
_____

What are you grateful for?

_____
_____
_____
_____

Friday:

On a scale of 1–10, how are you feeling today? _____

What do you need, want, or desire to get you one point higher?

_____
_____
_____
_____

What are you grateful for?

_____
_____
_____
_____

WEEKLY RECAP

What three things went well this week?

1. _____
2. _____
3. _____

What did I learn about myself this week?

_____
_____
_____
_____

What would I have done differently?

_____
_____
_____
_____

Which tips did I try this week?

_____
_____
_____
_____

What did I do this week that I would like to continue in the upcoming weeks?

_____
_____
_____
_____

JOURNAL ENTRY

Write a love letter to yourself.

_____
_____
_____
_____
_____
_____
_____
_____
_____
_____
_____
_____
_____
_____
_____
_____
_____
_____
_____
_____
_____
_____

WEEK 21

No Expectations

If you expect certain behaviors from others, you are likely to be let down. It is very rare for a person to behave exactly the way you want. It is burdensome to insist that people behave a certain way to meet your specific standards. These relationships are unfulfilling because they are based on judgment, not acceptance.

Imagine the burden-free and light feeling of not having to think about how others should act or respond. By letting go of the need to have others act in a way you deem appropriate, you will invite a lightness into your life and alleviate disappointment. Rid yourself of expectations and perfectionism and notice a greater sense of acceptance, contentment, and happiness.

Try these ideas THIS WEEK:

- Detach yourself from needing to be liked.
- Be compassionate.
- Open yourself up to criticism.
- Stop assuming.
- Give freely without wanting anything in return.
- Practice gratitude.
- Tell others what you appreciate about them.
- Be a master of your emotions.
- Write down what really matters to you.
- Rid yourself of perfectionism.
- Practice self-compassion.
- Reframe situations.
- Let go of comparisons.
- Focus on actions.
- Your idea: _____

✿✿✿✿✿   DAILY CHECK-IN   ✿✿✿✿✿

▪ Monday:

On a scale of 1–10, how are you feeling today? _____

What do you need, want, or desire to get you one point higher?

_____
_____
_____
_____

What are you grateful for?

_____
_____
_____
_____

▪ Tuesday:

On a scale of 1–10, how are you feeling today? _____

What do you need, want, or desire to get you one point higher?

_____
_____
_____
_____

What are you grateful for?

_____
_____
_____
_____

▪ Wednesday:

On a scale of 1–10, how are you feeling today? _____

What do you need, want, or desire to get you one point higher?

_____
_____
_____
_____

What are you grateful for?

_____
_____
_____
_____

▪ Thursday:

On a scale of 1–10, how are you feeling today? _____

What do you need, want, or desire to get you one point higher?

_____
_____
_____
_____

What are you grateful for?

_____
_____
_____
_____

▪ Friday:

On a scale of 1–10, how are you feeling today? _____

What do you need, want, or desire to get you one point higher?

_____
_____
_____
_____

What are you grateful for?

_____
_____
_____
_____

WEEKLY RECAP

What three things went well this week?

1. _____
2. _____
3. _____

What did I learn about myself this week?

_____
_____
_____
_____

What would I have done differently?

_____
_____
_____
_____

Which tips did I try this week?

_____
_____
_____
_____

What did I do this week that I would like to continue in the upcoming weeks?

_____
_____
_____
_____

\\\\\\\\\\\\\\\\\ **JOURNAL ENTRY** /////////////

Describe a time when your expectations weren't met but you still enjoyed the experience.

WEEK 22

Find What Makes You Feel Light

Have you noticed that certain people, places, or events make you feel heavy, exhausted, and drained? Maybe you've just attended a stressful event or were surrounded by negative individuals. On the contrary, have you noticed that certain people, places, or events make you feel carefree, sunny, and cheerful?

Make it your mission to find what makes you feel light! Do not give in to your bossy brain; remember few things are really that heavy! Surround yourself with people who radiate positivity, allow you to be yourself, and uplift you. Continuously find activities that align with your passions and give you inner peace. Find environments that give you joy, happiness, and comfort. Engage with activities, people, and environments that encourage laughter, bring out silliness, and make you feel happy.

Try some of these activities THIS WEEK:

- Watch a funny movie.
- Watch a funny video.
- Listen to upbeat music.
- Dance.
- Spend time in nature.
- Talk in a funny voice.
- Spend time with your favorite people.
- Spend time with animals.
- Take a walk.
- Practice a sport.
- Set a boundary.
- Read a joke book.
- Politely remove yourself from an uncomfortable situation.
- Dress up in bright colors.

✦ Play a game.

✦ Do karaoke.

✦ Make up a silly story.

✦ Your idea: _____

⚜⚜⚜⚜⚜ DAILY CHECK-IN ⚜⚜⚜⚜⚜

▩ Monday:

On a scale of 1–10, how are you feeling today? _____

What do you need, want, or desire to get you one point higher?

_____
_____
_____
_____

What are you grateful for?

_____
_____
_____
_____

▩ Tuesday:

On a scale of 1–10, how are you feeling today? _____

What do you need, want, or desire to get you one point higher?

_____
_____
_____
_____

What are you grateful for?

_____
_____
_____
_____

▪ Wednesday:

On a scale of 1–10, how are you feeling today? _____

What do you need, want, or desire to get you one point higher?

_____
_____
_____
_____

What are you grateful for?

_____
_____
_____

▪ Thursday:

On a scale of 1–10, how are you feeling today? _____

What do you need, want, or desire to get you one point higher?

_____
_____
_____
_____

What are you grateful for?

___

___

___

___

◼ Friday:

On a scale of 1–10, how are you feeling today? _____

What do you need, want, or desire to get you one point higher?

___

___

___

___

What are you grateful for?

___

___

___

___

WEEKLY RECAP

What three things went well this week?

1. _____
2. _____
3. _____

What did I learn about myself this week?

_____
_____
_____
_____

What would I have done differently?

_____
_____
_____
_____

Which tips did I try this week?

_____
_____
_____
_____

What did I do this week that I would like to continue in the upcoming weeks?

_____
_____
_____
_____

\\\\\\\\\\\\\\\ **JOURNAL ENTRY** ///////////////

Describe the part of your day that makes you feel light.

WEEK 23

The Reframe Game

Reframing our thoughts is a great way to change our perspective, shift our mindsets, and build up our happiness muscle! What would happen if we assumed that most people are coming from a good place? It really doesn't matter if they are or aren't—this exercise isn't for them; it's for you!

Begin by recognizing the negative thoughts and thought patterns. Next question those thoughts by asking if they are based on facts or assumptions. Finally begin to think about the opposite of that current thought. This empathic approach fosters an ability to look at things from a different perspective, see goodness in others, and ultimately cultivates happiness.

Try these reframes THIS WEEK:

- ✦ Feeling personally attacked by someone: That person is trying to help me in their own way.

- ✦ A friend cancels plans: They must be overwhelmed or busy.

- ✦ Someone is acting distant: They must have something stressful going on in their life.

- ✦ A person is rude: They must be having a bad day.

- ✦ Someone cuts you off while driving: They must be late for something very important.

- ✦ A friend gets off the phone abruptly: They have to do something that is time sensitive.

- ✦ An acquaintance doesn't say hi: They are preoccupied.

- ✦ That person gave me a dirty look: They saw something unpleasant on their phone.

- ✦ The person at the front desk was abrupt: They had an argument with a coworker.

- ✦ Your idea: _____

DAILY CHECK-IN

Monday:

On a scale of 1–10, how are you feeling today? _____

What do you need, want, or desire to get you one point higher?

_____
_____
_____
_____

What are you grateful for?

_____
_____
_____
_____

Tuesday:

On a scale of 1–10, how are you feeling today? _____

What do you need, want, or desire to get you one point higher?

_____
_____
_____
_____

What are you grateful for?

_____
_____
_____

▪ Wednesday:

On a scale of 1–10, how are you feeling today? _____

What do you need, want, or desire to get you one point higher?

_____
_____
_____
_____

What are you grateful for?

_____
_____
_____

▪ Thursday:

On a scale of 1–10, how are you feeling today? _____

What do you need, want, or desire to get you one point higher?

_____
_____
_____
_____

What are you grateful for?

_____
_____
_____

▪ Friday:

On a scale of 1–10, how are you feeling today? _____

What do you need, want, or desire to get you one point higher?

_____
_____
_____

What are you grateful for?

_____
_____
_____

WEEKLY RECAP

What three things went well this week?

1. _____
2. _____
3. _____

What did I learn about myself this week?
_____
_____
_____
_____

What would I have done differently?
_____
_____
_____
_____

Which tips did I try this week?
_____
_____
_____
_____

What did I do this week that I would like to continue in the upcoming weeks?
_____
_____
_____
_____

\\\\\\\\\\\\\\\\ **JOURNAL ENTRY** ////////////

Describe a mistake you made that turned out to be a great story.

WEEK 24

Judgy

The happiest people are the least judgmental ones. Having a mindset that embraces acceptance, understanding, and curiosity will ultimately foster happiness. When we choose not to judge, we become less burdened, less stressed, and less anxious. Once we relinquish our judgment of others, we understand that everyone is on their own journey with differing life experiences. This perspective fosters joy, appreciation of various perspectives, and happiness.

You can raise your awareness by observing your thoughts without reacting to them and acknowledging that everyone is on their unique path. By focusing on your own personal growth, you will foster a positive self-image, confidence, and happiness.

Try these tips THIS WEEK:

- Read a book/article about a different culture.
- Don't make comparisons.
- Research different customs.
- Go to a restaurant of a different cuisine.
- Go to a museum.
- Watch a documentary.
- Read a biography.
- Challenge stereotypes.
- Practice empathy.
- Increase self-awareness.
- Avoid projecting your baggage.
- Challenge assumptions.
- Think of opposite perspectives.
- Acknowledge that you do not know the full story.
- Notice your triggers.
- Flip the script on your judgments (reframe it).
- Remind yourself that everyone is doing their best.
- Your idea: _____

DAILY CHECK-IN

▪ Monday:

On a scale of 1–10, how are you feeling today? _____

What do you need, want, or desire to get you one point higher?

_____
_____
_____
_____

What are you grateful for?

_____
_____
_____
_____

▪ Tuesday:

On a scale of 1–10, how are you feeling today? _____

What do you need, want, or desire to get you one point higher?

_____
_____
_____
_____

What are you grateful for?

_____
_____
_____
_____

Wednesday:

On a scale of 1–10, how are you feeling today? _____

What do you need, want, or desire to get you one point higher?

_____
_____
_____
_____

What are you grateful for?

_____
_____
_____
_____

Thursday:

On a scale of 1–10, how are you feeling today? _____

What do you need, want, or desire to get you one point higher?

_____
_____
_____
_____

What are you grateful for?

_____
_____
_____
_____

Friday:

On a scale of 1–10, how are you feeling today? _____

What do you need, want, or desire to get you one point higher?

_____
_____
_____
_____

What are you grateful for?

_____
_____
_____
_____

WEEKLY RECAP

What three things went well this week?

1. _____
2. _____
3. _____

What did I learn about myself this week?

_____
_____
_____
_____

What would I have done differently?

_____
_____
_____
_____

Which tips did I try this week?

_____
_____
_____
_____

What did I do this week that I would like to continue in the upcoming weeks?

_____
_____
_____
_____

\\\\\\\\\\\\\\\\ **JOURNAL ENTRY** ////////////////

Describe how passing judgment makes you feel.

___

WEEK 25

Volunteer

*E*motional fulfillment, personal growth, and social connections are all ways that facilitate happiness. One of the best ways to do this is to volunteer! Volunteering fosters a sense of achievement, purpose, and happiness. Here is a huge secret: as much as volunteering helps others, the largest benefit comes to the person who is doing the volunteering. Volunteering negates loneliness, forces structure, and nurtures a hopeful mindset, all of which are a great foundation for happiness.

Force yourself to focus on something greater than yourself. By shifting your attention away from personal concerns, you begin to notice the beautiful tapestry of humanity. As you contribute time and energy into helping others, you will notice a sense of joy, fulfillment, and happiness.

Volunteer for one of these THIS WEEK:

- Animal shelter
- Food bank
- Library
- A friend in need
- A school
- A garden
- A homeless shelter
- A museum
- A neighbor
- A new mother
- An assisted-living facility
- A park
- A hospital
- Your neighborhood
- A nonprofit organization
- An elderly relative
- A beach cleanup
- A donation center
- A religious establishment
- A youth center
- Your idea: _____

👑👑👑👑👑 DAILY CHECK-IN 👑👑👑👑👑

▪ Monday:

On a scale of 1–10, how are you feeling today? _____

What do you need, want, or desire to get you one point higher?

_____
_____
_____
_____

What are you grateful for?

_____
_____
_____
_____

▪ Tuesday:

On a scale of 1–10, how are you feeling today? _____

What do you need, want, or desire to get you one point higher?

_____
_____
_____
_____

What are you grateful for?

_____
_____
_____
_____

▪ Wednesday:

On a scale of 1–10, how are you feeling today? _____

What do you need, want, or desire to get you one point higher?

_____
_____
_____
_____

What are you grateful for?

_____
_____
_____
_____

▪ Thursday:

On a scale of 1–10, how are you feeling today? _____

What do you need, want, or desire to get you one point higher?

_____
_____
_____
_____

What are you grateful for?

___

___

___

___

▪ Friday:

On a scale of 1–10, how are you feeling today? _____

What do you need, want, or desire to get you one point higher?

___

___

___

___

What are you grateful for?

___

___

___

___

WEEKLY RECAP

What three things went well this week?

1. _____
2. _____
3. _____

What did I learn about myself this week?

_____
_____
_____
_____

What would I have done differently?

_____
_____
_____
_____

Which tips did I try this week?

_____
_____
_____
_____

What did I do this week that I would like to continue in the upcoming weeks?

_____
_____
_____
_____

\\\\\\\\\\\\\\\ **JOURNAL ENTRY** ///////////////

Describe something that made you smile today.

WEEK 26

You Are Not Your Thoughts

Thoughts are fleeting and sometimes influenced by undesirable emotions, negative circumstances, or unworthy people. It is very important to disengage from these negative thought patterns because they contribute to self-doubt, fear, and unhappiness. Consider that you have about 8,000 thoughts each day; be mindful to not allow the negative ones to define you.

Shift your perspective as you acknowledge your thoughts, do not get attached to them, and remind yourself that a thought is not reality. Listen to your thoughts with curiosity, skepticism, and questions. This healthier, kinder, and more compassionate way of treating thoughts will enable you to have greater emotion regulation, fewer limiting beliefs, and improved happiness.

Try these strategies THIS WEEK:

- Visualize your thoughts as clouds coming and going.
- Observe your thoughts as an outsider.
- Set a daily intention.
- Limit comparisons.
- Use affirmations.
- Identify limiting beliefs.
- Practice self-compassion.
- Respond instead of react.
- Engage in grounding techniques.
- State the opposite of the current thought.
- Practice meditation.
- Change the script.
- Dismiss an "all-or-nothing" view.
- Engage in a growth mindset.
- Engage in routines.
- Journal.
- Your idea: _____

✣✣✣✣✣ DAILY CHECK-IN ✣✣✣✣✣

▪ Monday:

On a scale of 1–10, how are you feeling today? _____

What do you need, want, or desire to get you one point higher?

_____
_____
_____
_____

What are you grateful for?

_____
_____
_____
_____

▪ Tuesday:

On a scale of 1–10, how are you feeling today? _____

What do you need, want, or desire to get you one point higher?

_____
_____
_____
_____

What are you grateful for?

___

▪ Wednesday:

On a scale of 1–10, how are you feeling today? _____

What do you need, want, or desire to get you one point higher?

___

What are you grateful for?

___

▪ Thursday:

On a scale of 1–10, how are you feeling today? _____

What do you need, want, or desire to get you one point higher?

___

What are you grateful for?

_____
_____
_____
_____

▪ Friday:

On a scale of 1–10, how are you feeling today? _____

What do you need, want, or desire to get you one point higher?

_____
_____
_____
_____

What are you grateful for?

_____
_____
_____
_____

WEEKLY RECAP

What three things went well this week?

1. _____
2. _____
3. _____

What did I learn about myself this week?

_____
_____
_____
_____

What would I have done differently?

_____
_____
_____
_____

Which tips did I try this week?

_____
_____
_____
_____

What did I do this week that I would like to continue in the upcoming weeks?

_____
_____
_____
_____

\\\\\\\\\\\\\\\ **JOURNAL ENTRY** ///////////////

When have you felt most overwhelmed by your thoughts?

_____
_____
_____
_____
_____
_____
_____
_____
_____
_____
_____
_____
_____
_____
_____
_____
_____
_____
_____
_____
_____
_____

WEEK 27

Visualization

Visualization is a wonderful way to promote happiness by immersing your mind in positive thoughts, encounters, and experiences. The ritual of visualizing happy, safe, and beautiful scenarios will release endorphins in the body, which trigger happiness. It also creates feelings of hopefulness, optimism, and possibility.

Every person's visualization is different, so make yours personal to you. In your mind's eye, use you five senses to create visualizations that are as enticing, captivating, and appealing as you can. Use the power of your mind to get happy!

Try some of these visualizations THIS WEEK:

- ✦ Safe space visualization
- ✦ Joyful future visualization
- ✦ Success visualization
- ✦ Nature visualization
- ✦ Beach visualization
- ✦ Winter wonderland visualization
- ✦ Take a trip visualization
- ✦ Future positive relationship visualization
- ✦ Completion of a task visualization
- ✦ Event visualization
- ✦ Job visualization
- ✦ Gratitude visualization
- ✦ Your idea: _____

⚜⚜⚜⚜⚜⚜ DAILY CHECK-IN ⚜⚜⚜⚜⚜⚜

▪ Monday:

On a scale of 1–10, how are you feeling today? _____

What do you need, want, or desire to get you one point higher?

_____
_____
_____
_____

What are you grateful for?

_____
_____
_____
_____

▪ Tuesday:

On a scale of 1–10, how are you feeling today? _____

What do you need, want, or desire to get you one point higher?

_____
_____
_____
_____

What are you grateful for?

_____
_____
_____
_____

■ Wednesday:

On a scale of 1–10, how are you feeling today? _____

What do you need, want, or desire to get you one point higher?

_____
_____
_____
_____

What are you grateful for?

_____
_____
_____
_____

■ Thursday:

On a scale of 1–10, how are you feeling today? _____

What do you need, want, or desire to get you one point higher?

_____
_____
_____
_____

What are you grateful for?

_____
_____
_____
_____

▪ Friday:

On a scale of 1–10, how are you feeling today? _____

What do you need, want, or desire to get you one point higher?

_____
_____
_____
_____

What are you grateful for?

_____
_____
_____
_____

WEEKLY RECAP

What three things went well this week?

1. _____
2. _____
3. _____

What did I learn about myself this week?

_____
_____
_____
_____

What would I have done differently?

_____
_____
_____
_____

Which tips did I try this week?

_____
_____
_____
_____

What did I do this week that I would like to continue in the upcoming weeks?

_____
_____
_____
_____

\\\\\\\\\\\\\\\\ **JOURNAL ENTRY** ////////////

Describe your safe space in detail using your five senses.

___
___
___
___
___
___
___
___
___
___
___
___
___
___
___
___
___
___
___

WEEK 28

Forgiveness

When we release negativity and choose forgiveness, we open ourselves up to positivity and happiness. Holding on to anger, hurt, and resentment doesn't affect the other person at all, but it wreaks havoc on us. Harboring negativity is exhausting, emotionally draining, and actually quite unbecoming.

Why continue to punish yourself? Free yourself from grudges, pain of years past, and stale energy. Forgiveness is a choice, but also a gift to yourself. Reclaim your power.

Practice forgiveness THIS WEEK:

- Write a letter forgiving someone without sending it.
- Journal about forgiving someone.
- Identify the hurt.
- Allow yourself to feel.
- Forgive yourself.
- Empathize.
- Feel compassion.
- Speak out loud in private your forgiveness.
- Name your feeling and be compassionate with yourself.
- Reframe your perspective.
- Quit the blame game.
- Send love and light to that person.
- Your idea: _____

᚛᚛᚛᚛᚛᚛ DAILY CHECK-IN ᚛᚛᚛᚛᚛᚛

▪ Monday:

On a scale of 1–10, how are you feeling today? _____

What do you need, want, or desire to get you one point higher?

_____
_____
_____
_____

What are you grateful for?

_____
_____
_____
_____

▪ Tuesday:

On a scale of 1–10, how are you feeling today? _____

What do you need, want, or desire to get you one point higher?

_____
_____
_____
_____

What are you grateful for?

_____
_____
_____
_____

▪ Wednesday:

On a scale of 1–10, how are you feeling today? _____

What do you need, want, or desire to get you one point higher?

_____
_____
_____
_____

What are you grateful for?

_____
_____
_____
_____

▪ Thursday:

On a scale of 1–10, how are you feeling today? _____

What do you need, want, or desire to get you one point higher?

_____
_____
_____
_____

What are you grateful for?

_____
_____
_____
_____

▪ Friday:

On a scale of 1–10, how are you feeling today? _____

What do you need, want, or desire to get you one point higher?

_____
_____
_____
_____

What are you grateful for?

_____
_____
_____
_____

WEEKLY RECAP

What three things went well this week?

1. _____
2. _____
3. _____

What did I learn about myself this week?

_____
_____
_____
_____

What would I have done differently?

_____
_____
_____
_____

Which tips did I try this week?

_____
_____
_____
_____

What did I do this week that I would like to continue in the upcoming weeks?

_____
_____
_____
_____

FORGIVENESS

\\\\\\\\\\\\\\\\\ **JOURNAL ENTRY** /////////////

Describe how it feels to forgive someone.

WEEK 29

Morning Routine

With a proper morning routine in place, we can navigate challenges with less stress and anxiety. It also sets a tone of intent and purpose, as well as possibility and hope for the day. Having predictability and control in our morning routine fosters a relaxed mind, boosts self-esteem, and promotes happiness.

Set yourself up for success each and every day by prioritizing your morning routine. When you establish a nonnegotiable morning routine, you will be better able to navigate the unexpected uncertainties of the day ahead. By having a positive morning routine, you are taking control of your schedule, instead of your schedule taking control of you.

Try some of these in your morning routine THIS WEEK:

- Wake up 15 minutes earlier.
- Drink a glass of water.
- State three things you are grateful for.
- Meditate.
- Stretch.
- Do yoga.
- Exercise.
- Read.
- Journal.
- Eat a healthy breakfast.
- Tell yourself 5 positive affirmations.
- Outline your day.
- Text a loved one.
- Your idea: _____

ꙮꙮꙮꙮꙮꙮ DAILY CHECK-IN ꙮꙮꙮꙮꙮꙮ

▪ Monday:

On a scale of 1–10, how are you feeling today? _____

What do you need, want, or desire to get you one point higher?

_____
_____
_____
_____

What are you grateful for?

_____
_____
_____
_____

▪ Tuesday:

On a scale of 1–10, how are you feeling today? _____

What do you need, want, or desire to get you one point higher?

_____
_____
_____
_____

What are you grateful for?

_____
_____
_____
_____

▪ Wednesday:

On a scale of 1–10, how are you feeling today? _____

What do you need, want, or desire to get you one point higher?

_____
_____
_____
_____

What are you grateful for?

_____
_____
_____
_____

▪ Thursday:

On a scale of 1–10, how are you feeling today? _____

What do you need, want, or desire to get you one point higher?

_____
_____
_____
_____

What are you grateful for?

_____
_____
_____
_____

▪ Friday:

On a scale of 1–10, how are you feeling today? _____

What do you need, want, or desire to get you one point higher?

_____
_____
_____
_____

What are you grateful for?

_____
_____
_____
_____

WEEKLY RECAP

What three things went well this week?

1. _____
2. _____
3. _____

What did I learn about myself this week?

_____
_____
_____
_____

What would I have done differently?

_____
_____
_____
_____

Which tips did I try this week?

_____
_____
_____
_____

What did I do this week that I would like to continue in the upcoming weeks?

_____
_____
_____
_____

\\\\\\\\\\\\\\\\ **JOURNAL ENTRY** ////////////////

What positive impacts can you make in the day ahead?

___
___
___
___
___
___
___
___
___
___
___
___
___
___
___
___
___
___
___
___
___

WEEK 30

Nighttime Routine

A structured nighttime routine helps you sleep better so you feel rested the next day. A sense of tranquility as the night comes to a close fosters a comfortable, relaxed, and peaceful state. It is important to have a nighttime routine that promotes physical and mental relaxation, which alleviates stress and worry and promotes restful sleep.

It is important to provide yourself with a calming and restorative close to your day. Gradually shift your mind from stressors and responsibilities to peacefulness and relaxation. Having specific nightly rituals will promote structure, well-being, and happiness.

Try some of these nightly rituals THIS WEEK:

- Set out your clothes for the next day.
- Pack your lunch for the next day.
- Lower the lights.
- Lower the thermometer.
- Disconnect from screens.
- Take a warm bath.
- Journal.
- Read.
- Meditate.
- Use aromatherapy.
- Skin care/massage.
- Light stretching.
- Listening to soft music or sounds.
- Deep-breathing activities.
- Muscle-relaxation activities.
- Block out noise.
- Block out light.
- Set intentions for the next day.
- Practice gratitude.
- Be consistent.
- Your idea: _____

༄༄༄༄༄༄ DAILY CHECK-IN ༄༄༄༄༄༄

▪ Monday:

On a scale of 1–10, how are you feeling today? _____

What do you need, want, or desire to get you one point higher?

_____
_____
_____
_____

What are you grateful for?

_____
_____
_____
_____

▪ Tuesday:

On a scale of 1–10, how are you feeling today? _____

What do you need, want, or desire to get you one point higher?

_____
_____
_____
_____

What are you grateful for?

_____
_____
_____
_____

▪ Wednesday:

On a scale of 1–10, how are you feeling today? _____

What do you need, want, or desire to get you one point higher?

_____
_____
_____
_____

What are you grateful for?

_____
_____
_____
_____

▪ Thursday:

On a scale of 1–10, how are you feeling today? _____

What do you need, want, or desire to get you one point higher?

_____
_____
_____
_____

What are you grateful for?

___

Friday:

On a scale of 1–10, how are you feeling today? _____

What do you need, want, or desire to get you one point higher?

___

What are you grateful for?

___

WEEKLY RECAP

What three things went well this week?

1. _____
2. _____
3. _____

What did I learn about myself this week?

_____
_____
_____
_____

What would I have done differently?

_____
_____
_____
_____

Which tips did I try this week?

_____
_____
_____
_____

What did I do this week that I would like to continue in the upcoming weeks?

_____
_____
_____
_____

\\\\\\\\\\\\\\\\\ **JOURNAL ENTRY** /////////////

What challenges did you face today and how did you navigate them?

WEEK 31

Gratitude

*P*racticing gratitude leads to improved mental health, overall well-being, and happiness. By shifting focus from negative thoughts to positive aspect of our lives, we are building our happiness muscle. It may seem easier to focus on what is lacking in our lives or something negative, but with daily practice we can reroute those neural pathways.

Notice the feeling you have when you express gratitude in your thoughts, in your writing, and in your actions. This feeling will help you foster resilience, raise your self-esteem, and elevate your happiness.

Try some of these gratitude exercises THIS WEEK:

- Say three things you are grateful for before going to bed.
- Say three things you are grateful for as soon as you wake up.
- Say three things you are grateful for in the middle of the day.
- Start a gratitude journal.
- Say thank you for (*fill in the blank*) to someone.
- Mention someone's kindness to a friend or family member.
- Practice gratitude meditation.
- Give someone a compliment.
- Actively listen to someone.
- Encourage someone.
- Write a note of appreciation.
- Write a thank-you note.
- Give a gratitude gift.
- Draw a picture of something you are grateful for.
- Start a gratitude scrapbook.
- Appreciate small things.
- Write a gratitude story.
- Ask someone what they are grateful for.
- Your idea: _____

❦❦❦❦❦❦ DAILY CHECK-IN ❦❦❦❦❦❦

▪ Monday:

On a scale of 1–10, how are you feeling today? _____

What do you need, want, or desire to get you one point higher?

_____
_____
_____
_____

What are you grateful for?

_____
_____
_____
_____

▪ Tuesday:

On a scale of 1–10, how are you feeling today? _____

What do you need, want, or desire to get you one point higher?

_____
_____
_____
_____

What are you grateful for?

_____
_____
_____
_____

▪ Wednesday:

On a scale of 1–10, how are you feeling today? _____

What do you need, want, or desire to get you one point higher?

_____
_____
_____
_____

What are you grateful for?

_____
_____
_____
_____

▪ Thursday:

On a scale of 1–10, how are you feeling today? _____

What do you need, want, or desire to get you one point higher?

_____
_____
_____
_____

What are you grateful for?

_____
_____
_____
_____

▪ Friday:

On a scale of 1–10, how are you feeling today? _____

What do you need, want, or desire to get you one point higher?

_____
_____
_____
_____

What are you grateful for?

_____
_____
_____
_____

WEEKLY RECAP

What three things went well this week?

1. _____
2. _____
3. _____

What did I learn about myself this week?

_____
_____
_____
_____

What would I have done differently?

_____
_____
_____
_____

Which tips did I try this week?

_____
_____
_____
_____

What did I do this week that I would like to continue in the upcoming weeks?

_____
_____
_____
_____

\\\\\\\\\\\\\\\\ **JOURNAL ENTRY** ////////////////

Describe a challenge in your life that you are grateful for.

___

___

___

___

___

___

___

___

___

___

___

___

___

___

___

___

___

___

___

___

___

WEEK 32

Nature Bathing

We have all heard that getting our vitamin D from the sun is extremely important and can contribute to happiness. Combine that extra vitamin D with nature bathing, and you'll be sure to engage that happiness muscle. Nature bathing involves being outside in nature while simultaneously focusing on the beauty around you. This practice is linked to stress relief, a release of endorphins, a connection to nature, and an increase in peace and happiness.

Nature bathing is a mindful meditation activity that requires immersing yourself in nature. It is important to focus on the sights, sounds, smells, and sensations around you while walking through a natural area of your choosing. If your thoughts start to shift or become negative, that's OK, just quickly notice the beauty around you while feeling your footsteps hitting the ground beneath you.

Go outside and try nature bathing THIS WEEK:

- Notice your footsteps on the ground.
- Listen to birds chirping.
- Notice the formation of the clouds.
- Smell the scent of the flowers.
- Notice the temperature.
- Listen to the flow of water.
- Hear the leaves rustle.
- Watch the animals.
- Feel the wind on your skin.
- Cherish the tall trees.
- Notice the colors around you.
- Enjoy the sunlight.
- Inhale the fresh air.
- Touch the soil.
- Notice the moss on rocks.

- ✦ Appreciate blades of grass.
- ✦ Admire the shapes in nature.
- ✦ Your idea: _____

✿✿✿✿✿✿ DAILY CHECK-IN ✿✿✿✿✿✿

▪ Monday:

On a scale of 1–10, how are you feeling today? _____

What do you need, want, or desire to get you one point higher?

_____
_____
_____
_____

What are you grateful for?

_____
_____
_____
_____

▪ Tuesday:

On a scale of 1–10, how are you feeling today? _____

What do you need, want, or desire to get you one point higher?

_____
_____
_____
_____

What are you grateful for?

_____
_____
_____
_____

▪ Wednesday:

On a scale of 1–10, how are you feeling today? _____

What do you need, want, or desire to get you one point higher?

_____
_____
_____
_____

What are you grateful for?

_____
_____
_____
_____

▪ Thursday:

On a scale of 1–10, how are you feeling today? _____

What do you need, want, or desire to get you one point higher?

_____
_____
_____
_____

What are you grateful for?

_____
_____
_____
_____

▪ Friday:

On a scale of 1–10, how are you feeling today? _____

What do you need, want, or desire to get you one point higher?

_____
_____
_____
_____

What are you grateful for?

_____
_____
_____
_____

WEEKLY RECAP

What three things went well this week?

1. _____
2. _____
3. _____

What did I learn about myself this week?

_____
_____
_____
_____

What would I have done differently?

_____
_____
_____
_____

Which tips did I try this week?

_____
_____
_____
_____

What did I do this week that I would like to continue in the upcoming weeks?

_____
_____
_____
_____

\\\\\\\\\\\\\\\\ **JOURNAL ENTRY** ////////////////

Describe your favorite season.

___

WEEK 33

Self-Care

It's no surprise that prioritizing emotional health through self-care will boost happiness. Intentionally focusing on, and understanding, our personal needs highlight our self-awareness. When we know what we desire in order to regulate our emotions, we become more resilient.

This resilience will enable you to respond with appropriate responses when you encounter life challenges. By regularly catering to your self-care, you cultivate joy, peace, and happiness. Remember, self-care is not selfish!

Try these self-care activities THIS WEEK:

- Read a book.
- Give yourself a facial.
- Get a massage.
- Take a walk in nature.
- Journal.
- Listen to music.
- Eat a delicious meal.
- Garden.
- Set a boundary.
- Do nothing.
- Watch a movie.
- Take a nap.
- Say no.
- Say yes.
- Get a manicure.
- Diffuse essential oils.
- Cook.
- Stretch.
- Your idea: _____

⚜⚜⚜⚜⚜⚜ DAILY CHECK-IN ⚜⚜⚜⚜⚜⚜

▪ Monday:

On a scale of 1–10, how are you feeling today? _____

What do you need, want, or desire to get you one point higher?

_____
_____
_____
_____

What are you grateful for?

_____
_____
_____
_____

▪ Tuesday:

On a scale of 1–10, how are you feeling today? _____

What do you need, want, or desire to get you one point higher?

_____
_____
_____
_____

What are you grateful for?

_____

_____

_____

_____

▪ Wednesday:

On a scale of 1–10, how are you feeling today? _____

What do you need, want, or desire to get you one point higher?

_____

_____

_____

_____

What are you grateful for?

_____

_____

_____

_____

▪ Thursday:

On a scale of 1–10, how are you feeling today? _____

What do you need, want, or desire to get you one point higher?

_____

_____

_____

_____

What are you grateful for?

_____
_____
_____
_____

Friday:

On a scale of 1–10, how are you feeling today? _____

What do you need, want, or desire to get you one point higher?

_____
_____
_____
_____

What are you grateful for?

_____
_____
_____
_____

WEEKLY RECAP

What three things went well this week?

1. _____
2. _____
3. _____

What did I learn about myself this week?

_____
_____
_____
_____

What would I have done differently?

_____
_____
_____
_____

Which tips did I try this week?

_____
_____
_____
_____

What did I do this week that I would like to continue in the upcoming weeks?

_____
_____
_____
_____

\\\\\\\\\\\\\\\\ **JOURNAL ENTRY** ////////////////

How would you spend your perfect day off?

___

WEEK 34

Take Up Space

At times in our lives, we may have been interrupted, told to talk less, or made to feel that what we had to say wasn't important. Just because someone said or did these things doesn't make it true! We must assert our presence; we have the right to exist fully in any environment we find ourselves in. By taking up space, we are reminding ourselves and others that we have worth, value, and importance.

You have the right to be seen and heard. Moreover, your thoughts, opinions, and views are just as important as anyone else's. Shrinking yourself or succumbing to bullying to allow for someone else to try to get the upper hand is so last century! When you take up space and assert what you need, notice how your anxiety subsides, your self-confidence increases, and your happiness skyrockets.

Try these THIS WEEK:

- Advocate for yourself.
- Clearly communicate needs.
- Make a list of your needs and wants.
- Practice assertiveness skills.
- Set necessary boundaries.
- Ask for what you need.
- Speak up at a meeting.
- Order what you want at a restaurant.
- Practice saying no.
- Continue speaking if interrupted.
- Limit your use of "I'm sorry."
- Limit accommodating others at your expense.
- Never downplay a compliment.
- Sit in the front of a room.
- State your opinion.
- Say no without apologizing.

- ✦ Talk about something you accomplished.
- ✦ Schedule you time.
- ✦ Your idea: _____

✥✥✥✥✥ DAILY CHECK-IN ✥✥✥✥✥

▪ Monday:

On a scale of 1–10, how are you feeling today? _____

What do you need, want, or desire to get you one point higher?

_____
_____
_____
_____

What are you grateful for?

_____
_____
_____
_____

▪ Tuesday:

On a scale of 1–10, how are you feeling today? _____

What do you need, want, or desire to get you one point higher?

_____
_____
_____
_____

What are you grateful for?

_____
_____
_____
_____

▪ Wednesday:

On a scale of 1–10, how are you feeling today? _____

What do you need, want, or desire to get you one point higher?

_____
_____
_____
_____

What are you grateful for?

_____
_____
_____
_____

▪ Thursday:

On a scale of 1–10, how are you feeling today? _____

What do you need, want, or desire to get you one point higher?

_____
_____
_____
_____

What are you grateful for?

_____
_____
_____
_____

▪ Friday:

On a scale of 1–10, how are you feeling today? _____

What do you need, want, or desire to get you one point higher?

_____
_____
_____
_____

What are you grateful for?

_____
_____
_____
_____

WEEKLY RECAP

What three things went well this week?

1. _____
2. _____
3. _____

What did I learn about myself this week?

_____
_____
_____
_____

What would I have done differently?

_____
_____
_____
_____

Which tips did I try this week?

_____
_____
_____
_____

What did I do this week that I would like to continue in the upcoming weeks?

_____
_____
_____
_____

\\\\\\\\\\\\\\\\ **JOURNAL ENTRY** ////////////////

Describe the most challenging thing you faced today.

_____
_____
_____
_____
_____
_____
_____
_____
_____
_____
_____
_____
_____
_____
_____
_____
_____
_____
_____
_____
_____

WEEK 35

Declutter

When spaces are cluttered, we tend to become overwhelmed, which leads to stress, anxiety, and unhappiness. Seeing clutter and unfinished tasks can cause visual chaos and overwhelm; this makes it difficult to focus on things that bring us joy. However, decluttered and simplified spaces are serene, peaceful, and inviting.

Surrounding yourself in clean and inviting spaces opens your up to creativity, positive productivity, and happiness. Engaging in mindfulness while decluttering will also promote a sense of engagement and purpose.

Try some of these de-cluttering activities THIS WEEK:

- Do a seasonal clean out.
- Clear off all surfaces.
- Do a digital declutter.
- Practice the "one-in, one-out" rule.
- Create a donation bag.
- Implement the one-year rule (If you haven't used it in a year, get rid of it).
- Clean out your closet.
- Make your bed.
- Clean the sink.
- Decide to keep, donate, or toss in 30 seconds.
- Vacuum your car.
- Get rid of all old magazines and newspapers.
- Shred any unnecessary paperwork.
- Recycle old electronics.
- Sort a junk drawer.
- Make sure everything has a home.
- Put dirty clothes in a laundry basket.

✦ Focus on the purpose and joy of each item.

✦ Declutter for 10 minutes a day.

✦ Your idea: _____

✣✣✣✣✣ DAILY CHECK-IN ✣✣✣✣✣

▪ Monday:

On a scale of 1–10, how are you feeling today? _____

What do you need, want, or desire to get you one point higher?

_____
_____
_____
_____

What are you grateful for?

_____
_____
_____
_____

▪ Tuesday:

On a scale of 1–10, how are you feeling today? _____

What do you need, want, or desire to get you one point higher?

_____
_____
_____
_____

What are you grateful for?

_____
_____
_____

◾ Wednesday:

On a scale of 1–10, how are you feeling today? _____

What do you need, want, or desire to get you one point higher?

_____
_____
_____
_____

What are you grateful for?

_____
_____
_____

◾ Thursday:

On a scale of 1–10, how are you feeling today? _____

What do you need, want, or desire to get you one point higher?

_____
_____
_____
_____

What are you grateful for?

___

▪ Friday:

On a scale of 1–10, how are you feeling today? _____

What do you need, want, or desire to get you one point higher?

___

What are you grateful for?

___

WEEKLY RECAP

What three things went well this week?

1. _____
2. _____
3. _____

What did I learn about myself this week?

_____
_____
_____
_____

What would I have done differently?

_____
_____
_____
_____

Which tips did I try this week?

_____
_____
_____
_____

What did I do this week that I would like to continue in the upcoming weeks?

_____
_____
_____
_____

\\\\\\\\\\\\\\\\ **JOURNAL ENTRY** ////////////////

How would you live in your space if there was less clutter?

___

WEEK 36

Go That Way, Not This Way

When we step outside our comfort zones, we cultivate richer, varied, and exciting experiences that can promote happiness. Doing things out of habit can become dull, boring, and possibly miserable. However, doing something new and out of the ordinary can reignite a sense of curiosity, excitement, and happiness.

By engaging in unfamiliar activities, you stimulate your creativity and problem-solving skills while simultaneously improve your self-esteem. You may even meet new people, learn new things, or see a differing perspective when you switch up your usual activities. Your newfound adaptability will promote a positive mindset, self-assuredness, and happiness.

Try these things THIS WEEK:

- Go to a different grocery store.
- Fill up at a different gas station.
- Take a different route to school or work.
- Walk a new path.
- Ride your bike in a different direction.
- Wear a color you never wear.
- Attend a cultural event you are not familiar with.
- Try a new fitness class.
- Order a type of food you've never tried.
- Try a new hairstyle.
- Explore an unfamiliar part of your city.
- Plan a trip to somewhere you've never been.
- Listen to a new podcast.
- Watch a foreign film.
- Go to a new coffee shop.
- Take up a new sport.

- ✦ Wake up 15 minutes earlier each day.
- ✦ Go somewhere alone.
- ✦ Your idea: _____

✤✤✤✤✤✤ DAILY CHECK-IN ✤✤✤✤✤✤

▪ Monday:

On a scale of 1–10, how are you feeling today? _____

What do you need, want, or desire to get you one point higher?

_____
_____
_____
_____

What are you grateful for?

_____
_____
_____
_____

▪ Tuesday:

On a scale of 1–10, how are you feeling today? _____

What do you need, want, or desire to get you one point higher?

_____
_____
_____
_____

What are you grateful for?

_____
_____
_____

◼ Wednesday:

On a scale of 1–10, how are you feeling today? _____

What do you need, want, or desire to get you one point higher?

_____
_____
_____
_____

What are you grateful for?

_____
_____
_____

◼ Thursday:

On a scale of 1–10, how are you feeling today? _____

What do you need, want, or desire to get you one point higher?

_____
_____
_____
_____

What are you grateful for?

_____
_____
_____
_____

▪ Friday:

On a scale of 1–10, how are you feeling today? _____

What do you need, want, or desire to get you one point higher?

_____
_____
_____
_____

What are you grateful for?

_____
_____
_____
_____

WEEKLY RECAP

What three things went well this week?

1. _____
2. _____
3. _____

What did I learn about myself this week?

_____
_____
_____
_____

What would I have done differently?

_____
_____
_____
_____

Which tips did I try this week?

_____
_____
_____
_____

What did I do this week that I would like to continue in the upcoming weeks?

_____
_____
_____
_____

\\\\\\\\\\\\\\\ **JOURNAL ENTRY** ///////////////

If you could change one thing in your life, what would it be and why?

WEEK 37

No Comparing

Is your bossy brain behaving negatively again? Comparing yourself to others only brews self-doubt, low self-esteem, and jealousy. These negative emotions tend to simmer and grow, leaving you feeling resentful, envious, and unhappy. Reframe those thoughts and remind yourself that we have no idea what another person's journey entails. It is also important to reiterate that a person's success has zero bearing on your success. Likewise, feelings of happiness for another's success ultimately will make you feel happier too.

When you stop fixating on achievements, appearances, and lifestyles of those around you, you begin to recognize your own special accomplishments. Shift your perspective by focusing on your individual strengths, accomplishments, and uniqueness. By embracing and loving your individuality, you make space for self-acceptance, self-love, and happiness.

Try these THIS WEEK:

- Celebrate each achievement.
- Set personal goals.
- Embrace your uniqueness.
- Limit exposure to negative influences.
- Avoid "what if" comments.
- Cultivate hobbies.
- Live according to your values.
- Notice how far you have come.
- Unfollow profiles and sites that do not bring you joy.
- Treat yourself kindly.
- Practice gratitude.
- Focus on your strengths.
- Remain positive.
- Do not criticize others.
- Ditch perfectionism.
- Love the journey.
- Your idea: _____

DAILY CHECK-IN

▪ Monday:

On a scale of 1–10, how are you feeling today? _____

What do you need, want, or desire to get you one point higher?

_____
_____
_____
_____

What are you grateful for?

_____
_____
_____
_____

▪ Tuesday:

On a scale of 1–10, how are you feeling today? _____

What do you need, want, or desire to get you one point higher?

_____
_____
_____
_____

What are you grateful for?
_____
_____
_____
_____

▪ Wednesday:

On a scale of 1–10, how are you feeling today? _____

What do you need, want, or desire to get you one point higher?
_____
_____
_____
_____

What are you grateful for?
_____
_____
_____
_____

▪ Thursday:

On a scale of 1–10, how are you feeling today? _____

What do you need, want, or desire to get you one point higher?
_____
_____
_____
_____

What are you grateful for?

_____
_____
_____

▪ Friday:

On a scale of 1–10, how are you feeling today? _____

What do you need, want, or desire to get you one point higher?

_____
_____
_____
_____

What are you grateful for?

_____
_____
_____
_____

WEEKLY RECAP

What three things went well this week?

1. _____
2. _____
3. _____

What did I learn about myself this week?

_____
_____
_____
_____

What would I have done differently?

_____
_____
_____
_____

Which tips did I try this week?

_____
_____
_____
_____

What did I do this week that I would like to continue in the upcoming weeks?

_____
_____
_____
_____

\\\\\\\\\\\\\\\\\ **JOURNAL ENTRY** /////////////

Describe what is currently going right in your life and why.

___
___
___
___
___
___
___
___
___
___
___
___
___
___
___
___
___
___
___
___
___
___

WEEK 38

Action = Happiness

When we fervently participate in activities, we experience a sense of purpose, fulfillment, and happiness. This active engagement pulls us away from negative thoughts and feelings and immerses us in the present moment.

When you are active, you achieve goals, which fosters confidence and self-esteem. Not only will action release endorphins, but action can also create social connections, both of which contribute to your happiness. A body in action stays in action, so let's continue this cycle of positivity and happiness.

Try some of these activities THIS WEEK:

- Plant a garden on your porch, backyard, and/or neighborhood.
- Create/join a book club.
- Design a school/work newsletter.
- Sign up for a charity walk/run.
- Join a march.
- Email a politician.
- Support a local business.
- Beautify your space.
- Become a mentor.
- Go to an art or food festival.
- Donate to a cause you support.
- Start a holiday donation drive.
- Clean your yard.
- Organize a back-to-school donation drive.
- Raise funds for a charity.
- Recycle.
- Donate to a food shelter.
- Pick up trash in your community.
- Go to local farmers markets.
- Organize a block party.
- Your idea: _____

♛♛♛♛♛♛ DAILY CHECK-IN ♛♛♛♛♛♛

▪ Monday:

On a scale of 1–10, how are you feeling today? _____

What do you need, want, or desire to get you one point higher?

_____
_____
_____
_____

What are you grateful for?

_____
_____
_____
_____

▪ Tuesday:

On a scale of 1–10, how are you feeling today? _____

What do you need, want, or desire to get you one point higher?

_____
_____
_____
_____

What are you grateful for?

_____
_____
_____
_____

▪ Wednesday:

On a scale of 1–10, how are you feeling today? _____

What do you need, want, or desire to get you one point higher?

_____
_____
_____
_____

What are you grateful for?

_____
_____
_____
_____

▪ Thursday:

On a scale of 1–10, how are you feeling today? _____

What do you need, want, or desire to get you one point higher?

_____
_____
_____
_____

What are you grateful for?

_____
_____
_____
_____

▪ Friday:

On a scale of 1–10, how are you feeling today? _____

What do you need, want, or desire to get you one point higher?

_____
_____
_____
_____

What are you grateful for?

_____
_____
_____
_____

WEEKLY RECAP

What three things went well this week?

1. _____
2. _____
3. _____

What did I learn about myself this week?

_____
_____
_____
_____

What would I have done differently?

_____
_____
_____
_____

Which tips did I try this week?

_____
_____
_____
_____

What did I do this week that I would like to continue in the upcoming weeks?

_____
_____
_____
_____

\\\\\\\\\\\\\\\\\\ **JOURNAL ENTRY** /////////////////

Describe a few acts of kindness you carry out today.

WEEK 39

Thank-You Note Journal

A journal is a private, personal record of anything you want to share. It doesn't have to be grammatically correct, entries can be short or long, and it doesn't even have to make sense! The thank-you note journal is a new spin on the regular journal because its goal is to promote happiness. We have learned that happiness can come from gratitude, being kind to others, and reframing our thoughts.

A thank-you note journal is a great way to cultivate gratitude, appreciation, positivity, and of course happiness. Being thankful shifts your mindset from negativity and worry to optimism and contentment. Each day write a long or short, sloppy or neat, silly or serious thank-you note in your journal. Remember, no one is going to see it but you.

Write notes to some of these people/things THIS WEEK:

- The sunrise
- A delicious beverage or favorite meal
- The sanitation worker or mail carrier
- An acquaintance
- Your home
- Your favorite blanket or cozy pillow
- Your favorite teacher
- Your pet
- Your sibling
- Your parents or grandparents
- An actor or favorite author
- The waitperson
- Your neighbor
- The person who held the door open
- Your favorite stuffed animal
- Your vehicle
- Your idea: _____

ꗷꗷꗷꗷꗷꗷ DAILY CHECK-IN ꗷꗷꗷꗷꗷꗷ

▪ Monday:

On a scale of 1–10, how are you feeling today? _____

What do you need, want, or desire to get you one point higher?

_____
_____
_____
_____

What are you grateful for?

_____
_____
_____
_____

▪ Tuesday:

On a scale of 1–10, how are you feeling today? _____

What do you need, want, or desire to get you one point higher?

_____
_____
_____
_____

What are you grateful for?

_____

_____

_____

_____

■ Wednesday:

On a scale of 1–10, how are you feeling today? _____

What do you need, want, or desire to get you one point higher?

_____

_____

_____

_____

What are you grateful for?

_____

_____

_____

_____

■ Thursday:

On a scale of 1–10, how are you feeling today? _____

What do you need, want, or desire to get you one point higher?

_____

_____

_____

_____

What are you grateful for?

___

▪ Friday:

On a scale of 1–10, how are you feeling today? _____

What do you need, want, or desire to get you one point higher?

___

What are you grateful for?

___

WEEKLY RECAP

What three things went well this week?

1. _____
2. _____
3. _____

What did I learn about myself this week?

_____
_____
_____
_____

What would I have done differently?

_____
_____
_____
_____

Which tips did I try this week?

_____
_____
_____
_____

What did I do this week that I would like to continue in the upcoming weeks?

_____
_____
_____
_____

\\\\\\\\\\\\\\\\ **JOURNAL ENTRY** ////////////////

Describe something you can do today that will lead to gratitude and happiness in the future.

___

___

___

___

___

___

___

___

___

___

___

___

___

___

___

___

___

___

___

WEEK 40

Bloom from Within

*J*ust as a seed blooms into a beautiful, fragrant, and unique flower, we can also bloom into the person we are meant to be. The act of blooming from within is an internal journey based in self-discovery, authenticity, and self-acceptance. This growth involves standing up to our bossy brain by eliminating negative self-talk, conquering our limiting beliefs, and dismissing our need for external validation.

Continue to bloom by having compassion for yourself, cultivating self-love, and appreciating your self-discovery. As this personal discovery continues, you will understand how those who are most authentically themselves are the happiest. This inner peace and beauty allows you to experience life with greater ease, fulfillment, and happiness.

Try these strategies THIS WEEK:

- ✦ Challenge negative self-talk.
- ✦ Limit comparisons.
- ✦ Journal.
- ✦ Surround yourself with positive people.
- ✦ Talk to yourself like you would speak to your best friend.
- ✦ Eat healthy foods.
- ✦ Maintain good sleep hygiene.
- ✦ Practice mindfulness.
- ✦ Be curious.
- ✦ Exercise.
- ✦ Free yourself of mental clutter.
- ✦ Trust your gut.
- ✦ Think quality thoughts.
- ✦ Create boundaries.
- ✦ Be forgiving.
- ✦ Develop a can-do attitude.
- ✦ Do more of what brings you joy.
- ✦ Your idea: _____

✧✧✧✧✧✧ DAILY CHECK-IN ✧✧✧✧✧✧

▨ Monday:

On a scale of 1–10, how are you feeling today? _____

What do you need, want, or desire to get you one point higher?

_____
_____
_____
_____

What are you grateful for?

_____
_____
_____
_____

▨ Tuesday:

On a scale of 1–10, how are you feeling today? _____

What do you need, want, or desire to get you one point higher?

_____
_____
_____
_____

What are you grateful for?

_____
_____
_____
_____

▪ Wednesday:

On a scale of 1–10, how are you feeling today? _____

What do you need, want, or desire to get you one point higher?

_____
_____
_____
_____

What are you grateful for?

_____
_____
_____
_____

▪ Thursday:

On a scale of 1–10, how are you feeling today? _____

What do you need, want, or desire to get you one point higher?

_____
_____
_____
_____

What are you grateful for?

_____
_____
_____
_____

▪ Friday:

On a scale of 1–10, how are you feeling today? _____

What do you need, want, or desire to get you one point higher?

_____
_____
_____
_____

What are you grateful for?

_____
_____
_____
_____

WEEKLY RECAP

What three things went well this week?

1. _____
2. _____
3. _____

What did I learn about myself this week?

_____
_____
_____
_____

What would I have done differently?

_____
_____
_____
_____

Which tips did I try this week?

_____
_____
_____
_____

What did I do this week that I would like to continue in the upcoming weeks?

_____
_____
_____
_____

\\\\\\\\\\\\\\\\ **JOURNAL ENTRY** ////////////////

Describe something you need to forgive yourself for.

WEEK 41

Make a Choice (to Be Happy)

Exciting news . . . happiness is obtained by our individual mindset and perceptions, not by external circumstances or specific people. So when we come across barriers or difficult circumstances, we can think of them as chances to grow, learn, and evolve. Deciding to go about our day with positive energy and a positive attitude will attract positive people to us.

Remember, energy is contagious so make it positive, optimistic, and happy. Making the choice to be happy each day isn't easy, but it's a conscious decision that will become more natural, attainable, and beneficial the more you practice it. As you shift in your energy, you will begin to notice a newfound appreciation, gratitude, and happiness that surrounds you.

Try these strategies THIS WEEK:

- Make the choice to be happy each morning.
- Wake up and say three things you are grateful for.
- Write in a gratitude journal.
- Journal positive things your heard throughout the day.
- Celebrate all accomplishments.
- Read an inspiring book.
- Eliminate negative media.
- Set achievable goals.
- Get a good night's sleep.
- Practice deep breathing while reciting a positive mantra.
- Speak kindly to yourself.
- Exercise.
- Practice a soothing skin-care routine.
- Write a "life-improvement" list.
- Journal a personal strengths list.
- Do not give others the responsibility to make you happy.
- Set boundaries with those who are negative.

- ✦ Find pleasure in small things throughout the day.
- ✦ Eliminate saying "What if?"
- ✦ Your idea: _____

☙☙☙☙☙☙ DAILY CHECK-IN ☙☙☙☙☙☙

▪ Monday:

On a scale of 1–10, how are you feeling today? _____

What do you need, want, or desire to get you one point higher?

_____
_____
_____
_____

What are you grateful for?

_____
_____
_____
_____

▪ Tuesday:

On a scale of 1–10, how are you feeling today? _____

What do you need, want, or desire to get you one point higher?

_____
_____
_____
_____

What are you grateful for?

_____
_____
_____
_____

▪ Wednesday:

On a scale of 1–10, how are you feeling today? _____

What do you need, want, or desire to get you one point higher?

_____
_____
_____
_____

What are you grateful for?

_____
_____
_____
_____

▪ Thursday:

On a scale of 1–10, how are you feeling today? _____

What do you need, want, or desire to get you one point higher?

_____
_____
_____
_____

What are you grateful for?

___

___

___

___

▪ Friday:

On a scale of 1–10, how are you feeling today? _____

What do you need, want, or desire to get you one point higher?

___

___

___

___

What are you grateful for?

___

___

___

___

WEEKLY RECAP

What three things went well this week?

1. _____
2. _____
3. _____

What did I learn about myself this week?

_____
_____
_____
_____

What would I have done differently?

_____
_____
_____
_____

Which tips did I try this week?

_____
_____
_____
_____

What did I do this week that I would like to continue in the upcoming weeks?

_____
_____
_____
_____

MAKE A CHOICE (TO BE HAPPY)

\\\\\\\\\\\\\\\\ JOURNAL ENTRY //////////////

Describe what happiness looks and feels like in your life.

___

WEEK 42

Find the Joy

Becoming our authentic self is the true key to happiness. One way to discover our authentic selves is to identify our personal joy. It is important to recognize what brings us joy and then seek it out in order to honor our authentic self and cultivate happiness.

Perhaps you've been too busy, stressed, or unhappy to figure out what truly brings you joy. Pay attention to events, pastimes, and people you surround yourself with. Notice if they bring you joy. Be intentional as you pursue activities that bring you joy and a feeling of lightheartedness. Finding joy is open-ended and forever changing so seek, cultivate, and find joy daily.

Try these strategies THIS WEEK:

- Watch the sunset or sunrise.
- Take a soothing bath.
- Engage in a luxurious skin-care routine.
- Make a vision board.
- Watch a funny clip, show, or movie.
- Listen to a funny podcast.
- Attend a concert, show, or festival.
- Travel.
- Make plans with friends.
- Discover a new comedian.
- Cook a delicious meal.
- Admire flowers.
- Cuddle a baby.
- Caress your pet.
- Make your bed each morning.
- Go to the ocean.
- Garden.
- Practice gratitude.
- Spend time in nature.
- Open your shades each morning.

- ✦ Set an intention for the day.
- ✦ Take pictures of things that make you happy.
- ✦ Your idea: _____

✤✤✤✤✤✤ DAILY CHECK-IN ✤✤✤✤✤✤

▫ Monday:

On a scale of 1–10, how are you feeling today? _____

What do you need, want, or desire to get you one point higher?

_____
_____
_____
_____

What are you grateful for?

_____
_____
_____
_____

▫ Tuesday:

On a scale of 1–10, how are you feeling today? _____

What do you need, want, or desire to get you one point higher?

_____
_____
_____
_____

What are you grateful for?

_____
_____
_____
_____

▪ Wednesday:

On a scale of 1–10, how are you feeling today? _____

What do you need, want, or desire to get you one point higher?

_____
_____
_____
_____

What are you grateful for?

_____
_____
_____
_____

▪ Thursday:

On a scale of 1–10, how are you feeling today? _____

What do you need, want, or desire to get you one point higher?

_____
_____
_____
_____

What are you grateful for?

_____
_____
_____
_____

Friday:

On a scale of 1–10, how are you feeling today? _____

What do you need, want, or desire to get you one point higher?

_____
_____
_____
_____

What are you grateful for?

_____
_____
_____
_____

WEEKLY RECAP

What three things went well this week?

1. _____
2. _____
3. _____

What did I learn about myself this week?

_____
_____
_____
_____

What would I have done differently?

_____
_____
_____
_____

Which tips did I try this week?

_____
_____
_____
_____

What did I do this week that I would like to continue in the upcoming weeks?

_____
_____
_____
_____

FIND THE JOY

\\\\\\\\\\\\\\\\ **JOURNAL ENTRY** ////////////////

Describe the best compliment you could give yourself.

_____
_____
_____
_____
_____
_____
_____
_____
_____
_____
_____
_____
_____
_____
_____
_____
_____
_____
_____

WEEK 43

People-Please... Pa-lease!

*S*hifting our focus from external validation to internal satisfaction furthers our happiness. It's worth reiterating that true happiness comes from being your authentic self without seeking any approval from others. Another added bonus of stopping our people-pleasing habit is added energy and time. In addition, we further develop boundary-setting skills, which enhances our self-worth, reduces stress, and nurtures happiness.

Without this need for approval from others and this added energy, you will be able to explore your individual needs and wants and ultimately find happiness. Notice how you begin to feel less stress and anxiety and more freedom and happiness when the need to seek approval from others is released. Take this additional time to prioritize you!

Try these activities THIS WEEK:

- Watch a YouTube video about assertiveness.
- Practice making decisions based on your personal preferences.
- Create a vision board.
- Take a break from social media to reduce comparison.
- Watch TikToks about setting boundaries.
- Detach from what you think others think of you.
- Practice self-acceptance.
- Say no.
- Learn about manifestation.
- Talk to yourself the way you talk to your best friend.
- Embrace all praise.
- Practice staying true to your authentic self.
- Set healthy boundaries.
- Prioritize yourself.
- Avoid over-apologizing.
- Your idea: _____

DAILY CHECK-IN

▪ Monday:

On a scale of 1–10, how are you feeling today? _____

What do you need, want, or desire to get you one point higher?

_____
_____
_____
_____

What are you grateful for?

_____
_____
_____
_____

▪ Tuesday:

On a scale of 1–10, how are you feeling today? _____

What do you need, want, or desire to get you one point higher?

_____
_____
_____
_____

What are you grateful for?

_____
_____
_____
_____

▪ Wednesday:

On a scale of 1–10, how are you feeling today? _____

What do you need, want, or desire to get you one point higher?

_____
_____
_____
_____

What are you grateful for?

_____
_____
_____
_____

▪ Thursday:

On a scale of 1–10, how are you feeling today? _____

What do you need, want, or desire to get you one point higher?

_____
_____
_____
_____

What are you grateful for?

_____
_____
_____
_____

▪ Friday:

On a scale of 1–10, how are you feeling today? _____

What do you need, want, or desire to get you one point higher?

_____
_____
_____
_____

What are you grateful for?

_____
_____
_____
_____

WEEKLY RECAP

What three things went well this week?

1. _____
2. _____
3. _____

What did I learn about myself this week?

_____
_____
_____
_____

What would I have done differently?

_____
_____
_____
_____

Which tips did I try this week?

_____
_____
_____
_____

What did I do this week that I would like to continue in the upcoming weeks?

_____
_____
_____
_____

\\\\\\\\\\\\\\\\ **JOURNAL ENTRY** ////////////////

Describe what your ideal life would look like in five years.

WEEK 44

What Can We Control?

Here's a secret: We can't control anything but our own thoughts and our own actions. We sometimes think we can control what other people do, what other people say, and how other people act. We can't, nor should we want to. When we put expectations and controls on others, we set ourselves up for disappointment and unhappiness. When we relinquish this idea of control, however, we open ourselves up to personal freedom, inner peace, and happiness.

Letting go of control and your expectations of others makes space for self-compassion, kindness, and happiness. It fosters resiliency, strengthens your ability to adapt to new situations, and builds a positive mindset.

Try these strategies THIS WEEK:

- Limit planning and overthinking.
- Do a spontaneous activity.
- Stay present.
- Embrace imperfections in yourself and others.
- Recognize how you feel.
- Notice what your bossy brain is telling you and find another thought.
- Avoid micromanaging.
- Think about why this is causing angst, then reframe it.
- Set a five-minute timer, and worry only until the timer ends.
- Counteract your negative thoughts with three positive ones.
- Do something active.
- Practice self-compassion.
- Your idea: _____

⚜⚜⚜⚜⚜ DAILY CHECK-IN ⚜⚜⚜⚜⚜

▧ Monday:

On a scale of 1–10, how are you feeling today? _____

What do you need, want, or desire to get you one point higher?

_____
_____
_____
_____

What are you grateful for?

_____
_____
_____
_____

▧ Tuesday:

On a scale of 1–10, how are you feeling today? _____

What do you need, want, or desire to get you one point higher?

_____
_____
_____
_____

What are you grateful for?

_____
_____
_____
_____

▪ Wednesday:

On a scale of 1–10, how are you feeling today? _____

What do you need, want, or desire to get you one point higher?

_____
_____
_____
_____

What are you grateful for?

_____
_____
_____
_____

▪ Thursday:

On a scale of 1–10, how are you feeling today? _____

What do you need, want, or desire to get you one point higher?

_____
_____
_____
_____

What are you grateful for?

_____
_____
_____
_____

▪ Friday:

On a scale of 1–10, how are you feeling today? _____

What do you need, want, or desire to get you one point higher?

_____
_____
_____
_____

What are you grateful for?

_____
_____
_____
_____

WEEKLY RECAP

What three things went well this week?

1. _____
2. _____
3. _____

What did I learn about myself this week?

_____
_____
_____
_____

What would I have done differently?

_____
_____
_____
_____

Which tips did I try this week?

_____
_____
_____
_____

What did I do this week that I would like to continue in the upcoming weeks?

_____
_____
_____
_____

\\\\\\\\\\\\\\\\ **JOURNAL ENTRY** ////////////////

Describe ways to focus on something you can control in overwhelming situations?

WEEK 45

Appreciation

By practicing appreciation, we are able to shift our focus from what we lack to what we have. This change in our mindset will positively impact our mood, well-being, and happiness quotient. As we mindfully recognize the small joys in our lives, we create a toolbox of positivity to draw upon.

When you begin to enhance your happiness through appreciation, you are able to truly cherish those things that are meaningful in your life while giving much less weight to things that do not matter. Also, when you express appreciation to other people, you strengthen your bonds with them and foster happiness.

Try these tips THIS WEEK:

- Savor your morning cup of coffee or tea.
- Acknowledge nature's beauty.
- Recognize the kindness of friends.
- Give specific praise.
- Bring doughnuts to work or school.
- Compliment others.
- Make something homemade for others.
- Write a thank-you note.
- Offer congratulations.
- Ask others how they are.
- Bring a friend or coworker a gift.
- Offer your help.
- Leave a positive note.
- Ask about a friend's culture.
- Acknowledge others.
- Be an active listener.
- Offer others extra encouragement.
- Your idea: _____

✿✿✿✿✿✿ DAILY CHECK-IN ✿✿✿✿✿✿

▪ Monday:

On a scale of 1–10, how are you feeling today? _____

What do you need, want, or desire to get you one point higher?

_____
_____
_____
_____

What are you grateful for?

_____
_____
_____
_____

▪ Tuesday:

On a scale of 1–10, how are you feeling today? _____

What do you need, want, or desire to get you one point higher?

_____
_____
_____
_____

What are you grateful for?

_____
_____
_____
_____

◼ Wednesday:

On a scale of 1–10, how are you feeling today? _____

What do you need, want, or desire to get you one point higher?

_____
_____
_____
_____

What are you grateful for?

_____
_____
_____
_____

◼ Thursday:

On a scale of 1–10, how are you feeling today? _____

What do you need, want, or desire to get you one point higher?

_____
_____
_____
_____

What are you grateful for?

_____
_____
_____

▪ Friday:

On a scale of 1–10, how are you feeling today? _____

What do you need, want, or desire to get you one point higher?

_____
_____
_____
_____

What are you grateful for?

_____
_____
_____
_____

WEEKLY RECAP

What three things went well this week?

1. _____
2. _____
3. _____

What did I learn about myself this week?

_____
_____
_____
_____

What would I have done differently?

_____
_____
_____
_____

Which tips did I try this week?

_____
_____
_____
_____

What did I do this week that I would like to continue in the upcoming weeks?

_____
_____
_____
_____

\\\\\\\\\\\\\\\\ **JOURNAL ENTRY** ////////////////

Describe a time when someone was kind to you.

___

WEEK 46

Focus on the Good

Does your mind tend to focus on the negative more than the positive? You can change that and rewire your brain with practice and dedication. Continue to train that bossy brain of yours. Begin to highlight your positive traits, family and friend's positive traits, even stranger's positive traits while ignoring anything negative that comes to mind. It may be hard and certainly will take practice, but see the positive in each situation you find yourself in.

Why be bothered with the negative? It doesn't make us feel good or propel us toward happiness. However, when we consciously seek out the good, we reinforce our ability to find joy, strengthen our resilience, and enhance our happiness.

Try these tips THIS WEEK:

- Notice all good.
- Savor laughter.
- Practice gratitude.
- Compliment others.
- Take value in others' knowledge.
- See others' good qualities.
- Find the silver lining in something.
- Notice positive intentions.
- Have an open and accepting mind.
- Believe in others.
- Actively listen.
- Appreciate individuality.
- Take value in other people's skills.
- Accept people for who they are.
- Appreciate others' talents.
- Value others' life experiences.
- Notice positive character traits in others.
- Your idea: _____

⚜⚜⚜⚜⚜⚜ DAILY CHECK-IN ⚜⚜⚜⚜⚜⚜

▪ Monday:

On a scale of 1–10, how are you feeling today? _____

What do you need, want, or desire to get you one point higher?

_____
_____
_____
_____

What are you grateful for?

_____
_____
_____
_____

▪ Tuesday:

On a scale of 1–10, how are you feeling today? _____

What do you need, want, or desire to get you one point higher?

_____
_____
_____
_____

What are you grateful for?

_____
_____
_____
_____

▪ Wednesday:

On a scale of 1–10, how are you feeling today? _____

What do you need, want, or desire to get you one point higher?

_____
_____
_____
_____

What are you grateful for?

_____
_____
_____
_____

▪ Thursday:

On a scale of 1–10, how are you feeling today? _____

What do you need, want, or desire to get you one point higher?

_____
_____
_____
_____

What are you grateful for?

_____
_____
_____
_____

▪ Friday:

On a scale of 1–10, how are you feeling today? _____

What do you need, want, or desire to get you one point higher?

_____
_____
_____
_____

What are you grateful for?

_____
_____
_____
_____

WEEKLY RECAP

What three things went well this week?

1. _____
2. _____
3. _____

What did I learn about myself this week?

_____
_____
_____
_____

What would I have done differently?

_____
_____
_____
_____

Which tips did I try this week?

_____
_____
_____
_____

What did I do this week that I would like to continue in the upcoming weeks?

_____
_____
_____
_____

JOURNAL ENTRY

Describe how you can make a positive impact on someone's life.

_____
_____
_____
_____
_____
_____
_____
_____
_____
_____
_____
_____
_____
_____
_____
_____
_____
_____
_____
_____

WEEK 47

Overthinking Won't Change the Outcome

Our bossy brains want us to believe that overthinking will help us have control in all circumstances. We could never play out in our minds' eye all the scenarios in any given situation; there are far too many variables at play. Overthinking creates a false sense of control, unnecessary anxiety, and unhappiness. Excessive overthinking can contribute to unrealistic worry and fear. The truth is, 99% of the things we worry and overthink about never happen. Why waste so much time and energy overthinking when we can pour that energy into being happy?

Here's a secret: You've made it this far, so you have a 100% success rate! You have the ability, self-confidence, and mental acuity to make good choices without overthinking. Trust yourself to let go of excessive thinking and embrace the present moment. As you practice this new mindset, you open yourself up to spontaneity, creativity, and happiness.

Try these tips THIS WEEK:

- Embrace uncertainty.
- Limit negative discussions.
- Avoid procrastination.
- Focus on what you can control: your thoughts and actions (that's it!)
- Limit perfectionism.
- Use positive affirmations.
- Have realistic goals.
- Accept imperfections.
- Focus on solutions.
- Challenge all negative thoughts.
- Engage in a healthy distraction.
- Practice deep-breathing techniques.

- ✦ Focus on the present.
- ✦ Accept and embrace uncertainty.
- ✦ Journal.
- ✦ Your idea: _____

❧❧❧❧❧❧ DAILY CHECK-IN ❧❧❧❧❧❧

▪ Monday:

On a scale of 1–10, how are you feeling today? _____

What do you need, want, or desire to get you one point higher?

_____
_____
_____
_____

What are you grateful for?

_____
_____
_____
_____

▪ Tuesday:

On a scale of 1–10, how are you feeling today? _____

What do you need, want, or desire to get you one point higher?

_____
_____
_____
_____

What are you grateful for?

_____
_____
_____
_____

◼ Wednesday:

On a scale of 1–10, how are you feeling today? _____

What do you need, want, or desire to get you one point higher?

_____
_____
_____
_____

What are you grateful for?

_____
_____
_____
_____

◼ Thursday:

On a scale of 1–10, how are you feeling today? _____

What do you need, want, or desire to get you one point higher?

_____
_____
_____
_____

What are you grateful for?

_____
_____
_____

▪ Friday:

On a scale of 1–10, how are you feeling today? _____

What do you need, want, or desire to get you one point higher?

_____
_____
_____

What are you grateful for?

_____
_____
_____

WEEKLY RECAP

What three things went well this week?

1. _____
2. _____
3. _____

What did I learn about myself this week?

_____
_____
_____
_____

What would I have done differently?

_____
_____
_____
_____

Which tips did I try this week?

_____
_____
_____
_____

What did I do this week that I would like to continue in the upcoming weeks?

_____
_____
_____
_____

\\\\\\\\\\\\\\\\ **JOURNAL ENTRY** ////////////////

Describe a day you felt carefree.

WEEK 48

Sleep Hygiene

Establishing a nightly, soothing bedtime routine has an enormous impact on mood, emotional well-being, and happiness. Some may say it is the foundation for happiness. Having good sleep hygiene helps us deal with daily stressors, fosters resilience, and nurtures a positive outlook.

When you prioritize sleep and have consistent sleep patterns, you regulate your internal clock. This helps you cycle sufficiently through each sleep stage. These sleep stages regulate your cognitive, emotional, and physical functioning. Remember, self-care and sleep-care are not selfish—prioritize you!

Try these tips THIS WEEK:

- Stay hydrated throughout the day.
- Exercise daily.
- Limit caffeine and alcohol.
- Listen to a relaxation app or podcast.
- Practice deep breathing.
- Limit or avoid naps.
- Practice muscle relaxation.
- Dim the lights.
- Turn down the temperature.
- Have a cup of decaffeinated tea.
- Avoid heavy meals before bed.
- Establish an evening skin-care and hygiene routine.
- Declutter your bedroom.
- Use a blackout eye mask.
- Avoid stimulating content.
- Create a sleep-friendly environment.
- Use earplugs.
- Keep your sleep schedule consistent.
- Practice visualization.
- Diffuse calming scents.
- Your idea: _____

✣✣✣✣✣✣ DAILY CHECK-IN ✣✣✣✣✣✣

▪ Monday:

On a scale of 1–10, how are you feeling today? _____

What do you need, want, or desire to get you one point higher?

_____
_____
_____
_____

What are you grateful for?

_____
_____
_____
_____

▪ Tuesday:

On a scale of 1–10, how are you feeling today? _____

What do you need, want, or desire to get you one point higher?

_____
_____
_____
_____

What are you grateful for?

_____
_____
_____
_____

Wednesday:

On a scale of 1–10, how are you feeling today? _____

What do you need, want, or desire to get you one point higher?

_____
_____
_____
_____

What are you grateful for?

_____
_____
_____
_____

Thursday:

On a scale of 1–10, how are you feeling today? _____

What do you need, want, or desire to get you one point higher?

_____
_____
_____
_____

What are you grateful for?

_____
_____
_____
_____

▪ Friday:

On a scale of 1–10, how are you feeling today? _____

What do you need, want, or desire to get you one point higher?

_____
_____
_____
_____

What are you grateful for?

_____
_____
_____
_____

WEEKLY RECAP

What three things went well this week?

1. _____
2. _____
3. _____

What did I learn about myself this week?

_____
_____
_____
_____

What would I have done differently?

_____
_____
_____
_____

Which tips did I try this week?

_____
_____
_____
_____

What did I do this week that I would like to continue in the upcoming weeks?

_____
_____
_____
_____

JOURNAL ENTRY

What did you learn today?

_____
_____
_____
_____
_____
_____
_____
_____
_____
_____
_____
_____
_____
_____
_____
_____
_____
_____
_____
_____

WEEK 49

Overcome Limiting Beliefs

Limiting beliefs can be faulty, yet deeply engrained, thoughts that dictate what we want, what we believe, and what we desire. These thoughts may have been formed in childhood, from past experiences, or because of a narrow worldview. Thankfully we do not have to believe our bossy brains, negative thoughts, or potentially limiting beliefs. We now know that we can, and should, question all our thoughts.

You have the power to dismantle narrative beliefs and open yourself up to new possibilities, personal empowerment, and authentic happiness. Confronting your bossy brain and challenging beliefs that no longer serve you gives you the freedom to unlock your true potential. Question those false narratives such as *I am not good enough, I don't deserve success, I am unlikeable, I can't do it, I don't deserve happiness, I'm not talented, I'm not smart enough, I'm not worthy of love,* and *I'm too old or too young.* Soon you will rid yourself of all barriers creating your authentic, happy self.

Try these strategies THIS WEEK:

- Notice any assumptions you make.
- Seek evidence that contradicts your thoughts.
- Think of the opposite of your current thought.
- Question the validity of your thought.
- Question if this is your authentic thought or something you heard.
- Practice critical thinking.
- Check your sources.
- Seek to understand.
- Listen without judgment.
- Actively find conflicting views.
- Reframe self-limiting beliefs.
- Limit your use of "always" and "never."
- Challenge your beliefs.

- Practice reframing your thoughts.
- Create alternative beliefs.
- Step outside your comfort zone.
- Your idea: _____

✣✣✣✣✣✣ DAILY CHECK-IN ✣✣✣✣✣✣

▪ Monday:

On a scale of 1–10, how are you feeling today? _____

What do you need, want, or desire to get you one point higher?

_____
_____
_____
_____

What are you grateful for?

_____
_____
_____
_____

▪ Tuesday:

On a scale of 1–10, how are you feeling today? _____

What do you need, want, or desire to get you one point higher?

_____
_____
_____
_____

What are you grateful for?

_____
_____
_____
_____

■ Wednesday:

On a scale of 1–10, how are you feeling today? _____

What do you need, want, or desire to get you one point higher?

_____
_____
_____
_____

What are you grateful for?

_____
_____
_____
_____

■ Thursday:

On a scale of 1–10, how are you feeling today? _____

What do you need, want, or desire to get you one point higher?

_____
_____
_____
_____

What are you grateful for?

_____
_____
_____
_____

▪ Friday:

On a scale of 1–10, how are you feeling today? _____

What do you need, want, or desire to get you one point higher?

_____
_____
_____
_____

What are you grateful for?

_____
_____
_____
_____

WEEKLY RECAP

What three things went well this week?

1. _____
2. _____
3. _____

What did I learn about myself this week?

_____
_____
_____
_____

What would I have done differently?

_____
_____
_____
_____

Which tips did I try this week?

_____
_____
_____
_____

What did I do this week that I would like to continue in the upcoming weeks?

_____
_____
_____
_____

\\\\\\\\\\\\\\\ **JOURNAL ENTRY** ///////////////

Describe a belief you may have that hinders progress and happiness.

_____
_____
_____
_____
_____
_____
_____
_____
_____
_____
_____
_____
_____
_____
_____
_____
_____
_____
_____
_____
_____

WEEK 50

Negativity-Free Diet

A negativity-free diet involves eliminating or greatly reducing negativity from our lives similarly to restricting unhealthy foods when we want to feel better. A negativity-free diet encourages us to become mindful of our thoughts, mindful of who we surround ourselves with, and mindful of activities we choose to participate in.

This activity will help you become aware of how negativity affects your moods, your energy, and your overall happiness. Soon you will notice the ease at which you are able to put up boundaries when something feels negative. Eventually you can replace those patterns of negativity with positive thoughts, positive activities, and positive people, leading to overall happiness.

Try these strategies THIS WEEK:

- Stop negative self-talk.
- Limit negative social media.
- Enforce boundaries with negative people.
- Avoid gossip.
- Use positive language.
- Limit complaints.
- Focus on solutions.
- Implement a can-do attitude.
- Reframe thoughts.
- Notice the good.
- Practice self-care.
- Express gratitude.
- Practice empathy.
- Repeat positive affirmations.
- Visualize the positive.
- Get active.
- Meditate.
- Your idea: _____

⚜⚜⚜⚜⚜ DAILY CHECK-IN ⚜⚜⚜⚜⚜

▇ Monday:

On a scale of 1–10, how are you feeling today? _____

What do you need, want, or desire to get you one point higher?

_____
_____
_____

What are you grateful for?

_____
_____
_____

▇ Tuesday:

On a scale of 1–10, how are you feeling today? _____

What do you need, want, or desire to get you one point higher?

_____
_____
_____

What are you grateful for?

_____
_____
_____
_____

▪ Wednesday:

On a scale of 1–10, how are you feeling today? _____

What do you need, want, or desire to get you one point higher?

_____
_____
_____
_____

What are you grateful for?

_____
_____
_____
_____

▪ Thursday:

On a scale of 1–10, how are you feeling today? _____

What do you need, want, or desire to get you one point higher?

_____
_____
_____
_____

What are you grateful for?

_____
_____
_____
_____

▪ Friday:

On a scale of 1–10, how are you feeling today? _____

What do you need, want, or desire to get you one point higher?

_____
_____
_____
_____

What are you grateful for?

_____
_____
_____
_____

WEEKLY RECAP

What three things went well this week?

1. _____
2. _____
3. _____

What did I learn about myself this week?

_____
_____
_____
_____

What would I have done differently?

_____
_____
_____
_____

Which tips did I try this week?

_____
_____
_____
_____

What did I do this week that I would like to continue in the upcoming weeks?

_____
_____
_____
_____

NEGATIVITY-FREE DIET

\\\\\\\\\\\\ JOURNAL ENTRY ////////////

Describe what your day would look like if you didn't have any negative thoughts.

_____
_____
_____
_____
_____
_____
_____
_____
_____
_____
_____
_____
_____
_____
_____
_____
_____
_____

WEEK 51

Be Present

Anxiety lives in the future and sadness lives in the past; however, happiness lives in the present. When our thoughts are anchored in the here and now, our minds are not encumbered with what might happen tomorrow or what went wrong yesterday.

When you fully engage in what is happening around you, a sense of calm, peace, and happiness begins to materialize. Existing in the present strengthens bonds with people, increases knowledge, and fosters resilience. The more time you spend in the present, the happier you will be! So practice turning off that autopilot and savor the moment.

Try these strategies THIS WEEK:

- Put your phone away during every meal.
- Turn off all phone notifications.
- Notice the texture all around you.
- Notice the warmth of the sun.
- Notice the sounds in nature.
- Play a board or card game.
- Take an exercise class.
- Notice the smells all around you.
- Notice the flavors of the food you are eating.
- Recall what your friend wore to school/work today.
- Enjoy the feel of water on your skin.
- Notice the movement around you.
- Practice grounding activities.
- Do a body scan.
- Practice mindfulness movement.
- Count the trees on your walk.
- Notice your posture.
- Do not multitask.

- ✦ Reflect on your day each evening.
- ✦ Focus on your breathing.
- ✦ Your idea: _____

✤✤✤✤✤✤ DAILY CHECK-IN ✤✤✤✤✤✤

▪ Monday:

On a scale of 1–10, how are you feeling today? _____

What do you need, want, or desire to get you one point higher?

_____
_____
_____
_____

What are you grateful for?

_____
_____
_____
_____

▪ Tuesday:

On a scale of 1–10, how are you feeling today? _____

What do you need, want, or desire to get you one point higher?

_____
_____
_____
_____

What are you grateful for?

_____
_____
_____
_____

■ Wednesday:

On a scale of 1–10, how are you feeling today? _____

What do you need, want, or desire to get you one point higher?

_____
_____
_____
_____

What are you grateful for?

_____
_____
_____
_____

■ Thursday:

On a scale of 1–10, how are you feeling today? _____

What do you need, want, or desire to get you one point higher?

_____
_____
_____
_____

What are you grateful for?

_____
_____
_____
_____

▪ Friday:

On a scale of 1–10, how are you feeling today? _____

What do you need, want, or desire to get you one point higher?

_____
_____
_____
_____

What are you grateful for?

_____
_____
_____
_____

WEEKLY RECAP

What three things went well this week?

1. _____
2. _____
3. _____

What did I learn about myself this week?

_____
_____
_____
_____

What would I have done differently?

_____
_____
_____
_____

Which tips did I try this week?

_____
_____
_____
_____

What did I do this week that I would like to continue in the upcoming weeks?

_____
_____
_____
_____

\\\\\\\\\\\\\\\\ **JOURNAL ENTRY** ////////////////

Describe some steps you can take to better care for yourself.

WEEK 52

Fake It Till You Make It

We have all been in situations that may have been uncomfortable, outside our comfort zone, or even scary. "Fake it till you make it" is an incredibly useful technique that helps to build confidence, reframes negative thoughts, and promotes happiness. As we consistently embrace and practice these new attitudes, actions, and behaviors, they become part of who we are and part of our authentic self.

Consciously acting as if you already have the qualities you desire creates a positive feedback loop. This loop is a circular relationship between positive emotions and positive behaviors. The trick is to act as if you already have these positive traits, which in turn reinforces and validates your behaviors. This positive feedback loop will motivate you to continue doing the originally uncomfortable or scary activity. Eventually, this newfound confidence feels authentic, leading to feelings of happiness.

Try these strategies THIS WEEK:

- Adopt confident body language (head held high, shoulders back, back straight, palms open).
- Maintain eye contact with others.
- Practice making decisions.
- Smile at others.
- Dress for success.
- Initiate small talk.
- Attend social events with intention.
- Act enthusiastic (even when exhausted).
- Emulate a role model.
- Engage in success-driven visualizations.
- Attend a networking event.

- Act as if you already have success.
- Create a success journal.
- Focus on solutions.
- Highlight your strengths.
- Project confidence.
- Practice speaking with confidence (do not end a sentence with a question).
- Be open to learn.
- Become "it."
- Your idea: _____

✣✣✣✣✣ DAILY CHECK-IN ✣✣✣✣✣

Monday:

On a scale of 1–10, how are you feeling today? _____

What do you need, want, or desire to get you one point higher?

_____
_____
_____
_____

What are you grateful for?

_____
_____
_____
_____

▰ Tuesday:

On a scale of 1–10, how are you feeling today? _____

What do you need, want, or desire to get you one point higher?

_____
_____
_____
_____

What are you grateful for?

_____
_____
_____
_____

▰ Wednesday:

On a scale of 1–10, how are you feeling today? _____

What do you need, want, or desire to get you one point higher?

_____
_____
_____
_____

What are you grateful for?

_____
_____
_____
_____

Thursday:

On a scale of 1–10, how are you feeling today? _____

What do you need, want, or desire to get you one point higher?

_____
_____
_____
_____

What are you grateful for?

_____
_____
_____
_____

Friday:

On a scale of 1–10, how are you feeling today? _____

What do you need, want, or desire to get you one point higher?

_____
_____
_____
_____

What are you grateful for?

_____
_____
_____
_____

WEEKLY RECAP

What three things went well this week?

1. _____
2. _____
3. _____

What did I learn about myself this week?

_____
_____
_____
_____

What would I have done differently?

_____
_____
_____
_____

Which tips did I try this week?

_____
_____
_____
_____

What did I do this week that I would like to continue in the upcoming weeks?

_____
_____
_____
_____

\\\\\\\\\\\\\\\\ **JOURNAL ENTRY** ////////////////

Describe characteristics you admire in others that seem confident.

Conclusion

Congratulations on reaching the end of your journey toward happiness! Take a moment to reflect on the amazing progress you've made over these 52 weeks. Each and every exercise was a step toward a deeper understanding of what happiness means to you. You have learned how to cultivate gratitude, nurture positive relationships, embrace mindfulness, reframe your thoughts, and discover what makes you happy.

Happiness is not a destination, but an ongoing journey. The tools you have learned throughout this book will continue to enrich your life and help you navigate life's ups and downs with ease. Revisit each entry if you need a boost or happiness reminder.

Thank you for allowing this book to be a part of your journey. Cheers to years and years and years of happiness!

About the Author

Stacie Boyar is a licensed mental health counselor with a master's degree in education as well. She is in private practice, specializing in anxiety, depression, and PTSD. Stacie lives in South Florida with her husband, two daughters, and two dogs. You can find her at www.namastacie.net, on Instagram at namastacie_boyar, and her podcast is Namastacie.

www.ingramcontent.com/pod-product-compliance
Lightning Source LLC
LaVergne TN
LVHW081537070526
838199LV00056B/3692